THE SERVICE AND
STATUS OF WOMEN
IN THE CHURCHES

THE SERVICE AND
STATUS OF WOMEN
IN THE CHURCHES

BY

KATHLEEN BLISS

WITH A FOREWORD BY
W. A. VISSER 't HOOFT

S C M PRESS LTD
56 BLOOMSBURY STREET
LONDON

First published 1952

*Printed and bound in Great Britain by
Tonbridge Printers Ltd., Peach
Hall Works, Tonbridge, Kent*

CONTENTS

FOREWORD

ONE of the 'Concerns of the Churches' which was discussed
at the first Assembly of the World Council of Churches at
Amsterdam in 1948 was 'the Life and Work of Women in
the Church'. The subject had been put on the programme because
a first inquiry on this matter had met with an extraordinary wide
and keen response and had made it clear that this had become a
vital issue in many countries. The amount of material which came
from the different Churches was so considerable that it was
impossible to produce more than a very provisional and short
report for the Assembly itself, and it was therefore decided that a
fuller report should be prepared.

But there are reports and reports. The 'Commission on Life and
Work of Women in the Church' which had been set up by the
World Council after the Assembly considered that what was
wanted was not a mere tabulation of the various national docu-
ments, but rather a personal interpretation of the situation as it
was revealed in the material. It therefore asked Dr. Kathleen
Bliss to present the facts together with her own evaluation of these
facts. The result is this highly illuminating survey of the place and
work of women in many Churches which may claim to represent
the first world-wide study on this subject which has ever been
made. The World Council of Churches must of course accompany
it with the customary phrase that the opinions which are expressed
in these pages are not necessarily those of the World Council
itself. But it must be added immediately, that the World Council
does not apologise for calling attention to this crucial aspect of
the situation of the Church in the modern world. It is not only the
opinion of Dr. Bliss, but the almost monotonous and impressive
Leitmotiv of the reports from all countries that (in the words of the
Amsterdam Assembly) 'the Church as the Body of Christ consists
of men and women, created as responsible persons to glorify God

9

and to do His Will', but that 'this truth accepted in theory, is too often ignored in practice'.

And let no one think that this is a mere matter of organisational adjustment, which can be put right by a little more imagination on the part of the masculine members of the Church. There is no doubt that more imagination is required, but the real question is whether the Churches have really faced up to the basic tenets of their own faith concerning the relationships of men and women in the fellowship of the Church of Christ.

The purpose of this book is not to offer solutions for the problems involved in these relationships. Its rôle is rather to show where the Churches stand to-day, at what points they may be able to learn from each other, and what questions need to be faced.

During recent decades the Churches have seen more clearly than they did before that it is not by borrowing ideas from the world, but by rediscovering the source of their own life that they find the most relevant word for these times. But they have not yet begun to apply this insight to any considerable extent to that great modern problem of the right relations between man and woman. This book will perform its true function, if it makes many Christians wonder whether we may not expect a great deal of new light and new strength in the life of the Church, if we begin to ask seriously what the will of God is concerning the diversity of gifts of men and women and concerning the one spirit in which they are to serve together their common Lord.

W. A. VISSER 't HOOFT,
General Secretary of the
World Council of Churches

PREFACE

THIS BOOK is written out of the responses to an enquiry initiated by the World Council of Churches into the present function and status of women in its member Churches. Replies came from nearly fifty countries. These reports varied very much in size and content. Some were prepared by inter-denominational committees which met many times, collecting and collating material; others came from countries where communications were poor, and consultation impossible. Some reports contained a wealth of detail, some only general statements; some gave the social context of the Church under review, others left the writer to find that out for herself.

By the kindly co-operation of a number of correspondents I have been able to make good many gaps. Where accuracy of detail and right assessment of all the factors were of great importance (as, for example, in describing the action of Churches on the ordination of women), what I wrote has been checked by persons in the country concerned who were in the best position to give all the facts. I gratefully acknowledge their help. I am equally indebted to those who translated both reports and additional material, especially to Dr. Olive Wyon, Mrs. Dorothea Barton, and Miss Evans of the World Council's staff, and to Miss M. A. Bryan, who prepared the index.

The method on which I have worked has been to select from the reports in such a way as to illustrate all the main types of the work of women in the Churches. Unless I have stated otherwise, all quotations are from the reports. Those who scan the index in the hope of finding a complete description of everything women are doing in any one of more than a hundred Churches and Christian organisations, will be disappointed. To produce a reference book of this kind would be the work of a large staff for some years: even the Churches themselves cannot supply statistics on more than a fraction of all the work of women going on under their auspices. The book is meant to be a general and, as far as possible, balanced picture of what is happening, what the problems are, and how they are being either met and overcome or left unsolved.

To the material contained in the reports I have made two additions. The half-dozen or so of the reports which sketched the historical origins of some women's work showed me how much light is shed on the present position by knowing how and why it came about. I have sketched the historical origins of some of the more important features of women's present place in the Churches. It also became clear to me that statements about the degree and kind of responsibility exercised by women in the Churches meant very little unless it could be in some sense compared with the place of women in society. In my first and last chapters I have therefore attempted a task which needs far fuller treatment, the interaction between Church and society, especially as it affects the rôle of women in both.

K. BLISS

November, 1951

I

WOMEN, CHURCH AND SOCIETY

WOMEN have always served the Church throughout its long history. The means by which that service was given has varied both with social custom and with religious thought. The content of that service has remained curiously the same down the ages. Occasionally a woman appears as a prophet, a mystic, an administrator, an artist—men of such calibre are rare, but women much rarer, whether from nature or from social conditioning, this is not the moment to argue. But *always*, whatever the social conditions, whatever the attitude of the existing Church authorities to women's place in the Church, large numbers of women have engaged in two tasks—the education of youth and the care of the sick, the poor and the aged. When she is not preparing syllabuses for Sunday Schools, and organising training courses for youth leaders as a director of religious education, the woman with a gift for educating youth and helping others to do the same is found building up a convent school. If social conditions or Church restrictions prevent her from such activities, she retreats into her base—the home—and there she is the transmitter of culture from one generation to another, the inculcator of morals and the teacher of the faith. So also the woman who in this generation labours for long hours in the church hall, spurring on her volunteers to sorting old clothes and rolling bandages, or sallies forth to visit in hospital and prison, has her counterpart in other times and places in the lady of the manor, brewing her herbal concoctions and cures and dispensing them at the kitchen door with good advice and godly admonition.

To say that women's powers to educate and to succour have found an outlet in an immense variety of ways is not the same thing as saying that the Church has made use of even a tithe of the vast reserve of talent and devotion which lay to hand in the persons of its women members. Often a woman's zeal has been damped down and discouraged by the Church, her gifts of mind and spirit refused, her devotion and labour frittered away on trifles. In 1852 Florence Nightingale wrote to Dean Stanley, an intimate friend, her own inner thoughts about the Church of England of which she was a member. She said: 'I would have given her my head, my hand, my heart. She would not have them. She did not know what to do with them. She told me to go back and do crochet in my mother's drawing-room. "You may go to the Sunday School if you like," she said. But she gave me no training even for that. She gave me neither work to do for her, nor education for it.' Other women have felt the same about their churches.

Yet the purposes of God in Florence Nightingale were not thwarted by the blindness of the Church of England to the service which women might have rendered. Clinging to her faith in her own inner call to relieve human suffering, she met nothing but failure in attempting in England to equip herself as a nurse. But when she was almost overwhelmed by despair the way opened for her to go to Kaiserswerth to the new and almost unknown mother-house of the deaconesses whom Pastor Fliedner was training, and in their hospital she learned. And this is only one of many examples of the essentially ecumenical character of any study of women in the Church, for when one Church loses all consciousness, apparently, of the very existence of women able and willing to serve, another Church or another branch of the same Church, is beginning to take action.

There have been periods in the life of almost all branches of the Christian Church in which women are honoured, when many are able to use their gifts in a variety of ways, and a few attain to great eminence in the Church. Such times are to be found in the Eastern Orthodox Church between the fourth and ninth century when numbers of women ordained by bishops to be deaconesses taught in schools and in congregations and when a small but significant number attained wide reputations for their scholarship, piety and Christian witness in martyrdom. Palladius describes the deaconess Sylvia who 'loved the divine Scripture and turned nights into days in order to read the writings of the exegetists'. Deaconess

Makrina, sister of St. Basil of Cappadocia, was a philosopher and theologian of no mean distinction. Phebronia had such a gift for explaining Scripture that 'the whole town of Nisibia gathered together to listen to her; everybody praised her scholarship'. Two deaconesses, Dominica and Mavra, opened the first school for Christian girls. Many suffered martyrdom and some, like Tatiana, Nonna, Olympiada, Xenia, Nina, Susanna and Irina were canonised by the Eastern Church. So great was the influence of women that Lucenius, in the last persecution, issued an edict forbidding men and women to worship together—not in the interests of morality but because of the great influence of women in the Christian movement. Nor did these women whose names are here mentioned (and there were very many others) work unofficially, with the Church authorities half disapproving and half tolerating their efforts. More than one Ecumenical Council discussed and regulated the work of women, and demanded a high standard of theological attainment,[1] and State laws of successive Emperors applied legal sanctions to breaches of discipline among deaconesses.

Women also had a high status in Anglo-Saxon Britain. Women, especially women of noble birth, were the first converts to the Christian faith and took up from the missionaries,.from whom they learned, the task of evangelising their tribes. It was Queen Bertha who made to St. Augustine and his followers the grant of land on which to build the cathedral of Canterbury: and many are the stories of tribal queens and princesses suffering martyrdom for the new faith. Soon religious houses for women were established in Anglo-Saxon England, and even mixed houses (separate departments of a single religious community). At the close of the seventh century there were five such mixed houses in Kent alone, all governed by women. In the councils of the Church the position of honour given to Abbesses was next to that of Bishops. St. Hilda presided at the great Synod of Whitby in 664, and five abbesses put their names to the Acts of the Great Council of Beckenham in 694.

It is easy of course to exaggerate the place occupied by women

---

[1] It should be pointed out that whereas in the West theology is almost always a study pursued by clerics, in the Eastern Church, by long tradition, the majority of theologians are laity, thus a woman studying and expounding the Scriptures would not be suspected of sacerdotal aspirations.

in the Church in past ages. The plain fact is that with rare, and for the most part modern exceptions, all clergy are men and the highest offices of the Church—all Churches—are occupied by the clergy. In saying that there have been periods when women have held a high and honoured place in the Church, it is not meant that down the course of history now men and now women have had the major share in shaping the course of the Church's life. That is not true. The guiding hands have always been masculine. But what is true is that at some periods women who have felt the call of God to serve Him and their fellows, have found a means of fulfilling that vocation in the Church and at other times the Church has had no room for them, no belief in their 'call', no encouragement and guidance in the fulfilment of it. Women have never found their place in the Church by imposing their will and their views: whether they find fulfilment or frustration depends on the relationship of the sexes—not only the relation of an individual man and an individual woman in marriage but the total relationship, governed by what men think of women, how they behave towards them and what women think of themselves. The question of the place of women in the Churches is not a 'women's question'. It might more truly be called a 'men's question'. Fundamentally it is a question of *relationship*.

This relationship between men and women on which fundamentally the status and the function of women in the Churches depend is never entirely fixed. There is always a tension between what comes to a Church from the Gospel and from the Church's own past history and tradition and what comes from outside, from society, where the economic, social and educational position of women is always changing. It is not a case of a fixed unchangeable Christian principle and Church tradition being in tension with changing social attitudes. Asked to give 'the Christian doctrine of the relation of the sexes', no Christian theologian could give a clear and concise answer. He would have to say that the Church recognises both an order of creation in which God created humanity male and female from the beginning and an order of redemption in which in St. Paul's words 'there is neither male nor female'. Far from there being any fixed Christian attitude or principle in this matter, the widest possible divergences of opinion have found expression in the Christian Church. Arguing from nature, some men in some ages have put woman in a completely subservient position to man—God made her the weaker vessel, a form of property, a source of temptation,[1] an earthy drag on the spirit of man. Arguing from grace, others have at times attempted to minimise or abolish altogether sexual distinctions in the Christian fellowship, only to find that the order of creation could not be set aside. Scripture texts could be found to prove almost anything about woman—except that she does not exist—and have been freely quoted down the ages.

Yet this sorry picture of inconclusive and acrimonious debate is not the whole truth. The times when the Church regarded women as a lower species, doubtfully redeemable, or as ignorant and ineducable, are always the times when the Church is dead in other matters—failing to evangelise, indifferent to human suffering. As soon as quickening life returns to the Church, or to some section within it, men and women are found working at the same enterprise and new attitudes begin to prevail. Thus the new life of piety and religion in the home which came to the German Church in the eighteenth century led on to the renewal of the order of deaconess and the spread of that great movement throughout Europe. Methodism, before ever it became a public movement, drew together men and women in the home for Bible study, prayer and the practice of a disciplined Christian life: the Oxford Movement which was primarily a liturgical and theological movement quickened the life of the Church of England and part of the recovery of the Catholic heritage was the re-establishment of Religious Communities for women, suppressed at the Reformation. Supremely the modern missionary movement brought about a minor revolution in the life of the Churches of Europe and of America, drawing women into its service and opening to them opportunities without parallel in the whole of Church history.

But the Church's conception of women, their relationship with men and their place in the Church, is affected by society. The Church is not a closed body sealed off from the influence of economic and social change or from the climate of thought

[1] To quote but one example: Women are 'a necessary evil, a natural temptation, a desirable calamity, a domestic peril and a painted ill'.—St. Chrysostom.

B

prevailing outside its walls. All the flux and flow of society is present within the Church in the persons of its members and the day to day life of the Church is deeply and often unconsciously influenced by ideas, habits and customs belonging to society at large or to other groups of persons and systems of thought. For example, the gospels and epistles clearly show that there is a place for ascetism in the Christian life and that some are called for Christ's sake to forego marriage and family life. But there was brought into the Church from Eastern cults a form of ascetism based on the doctrine that the flesh itself is evil. Couched in its extremer forms this doctrine was rejected by the Church as heresy. Eastern non-Christian conceptions of ascetism profoundly affected ways of thinking about women even among Orthodox Christians. As in India the sadhu, so in the Eastern Mediterranean area the Christian hermit or desert father was considered the holy man *par excellence*. Throughout the first centuries of Christian history, war was waged by the Church on the sexual laxity and perversion of paganism, but it was always in balance whether the ideal of marriage or the ideal of ascetic forebearance would be the Church's main alternative to sexual profligacy. Now one, now the other, now both were commended, but in the end the balance of opinion in the Eastern Churches tipped over in favour of the ascetic life as the ideal of the Christian life, with marriage as a commendable second choice for those who were incapable of the first. There was a good deal of abuse of women by certain ascetics as the source of sexual temptation, drawing men away from the pursuit of holiness. None the less, the 'widows' were almost an Order in the Church for some four centuries and were gradually replaced by 'virgins', who as deaconesses moved freely in the congregations (the Church of St. Sophia, Constantinople, alone had no less than 20 attached to it in the sixth century, at the disposal of the bishop). Whether these virgins ever broke out in abuse of men as a source of temptation to them in their vocation we do not know: if they did, their utterances have not been preserved. But the denigration of women had smaller effect than the tendency on the part of the ascetics to group themselves into monasteries and disappear from the world. At the same time the order of deaconesses declined, the holy women took themselves to nunneries, and nunneries and monasteries alike, sealed off from the life of the Church and the world, became inward-looking and sank gradually into inertia. The result of all this was, in the opinion of the very active lay orthodox group, Aktines, now flourishing in Athens, that the Church never held out to lay people (including of course *all* women) an ideal of a Christian way of life in the world. 'The man who kept awake all night praying in Church never understood the man who was kept awake at night by his crying baby, even though that baby might be a St. Basil.' Not only did the ascetic and the Christian layman not understand each other, they could not influence each other. The vigour of lay initiative and the superb work of women in some of the Orthodox Churches today may well be a centuries-old reaction against the capitulation of the Church to a non-Christian ideal of man-woman relationships.

It would be possible, and might be profitable, to show how in other ways, and at other times, ideas and customs prevalent outside the Church have influenced the Church's attitude to women. The irruption of Islam, for example, over the Straits of Gibraltar into Spain in the seventh century, following the obliteration of Christian Asia Minor, Syria and North Africa by Arab invaders, opened up the whole Mediterranean world to Islamic influences. Arabic culture, mathematics, philosophy seeped into the Mediterranean world, and with them the Islamic view of woman as an object of sexual satisfaction and a form of property. But this trough was succeeded by another wave. Not by any direct action of Church authorities, but out of the distress of the times, against which Christian secular rulers battled, there arose the ideal of chivalry, the conception of the Christian king, as protector of the weak and dispenser of justice, of the Christian knight, and of the pure maiden and the good woman. Such a history of rises and falls, of periods when women were honoured followed by times when their place both in society and in the Church was hardly more than that of chattel, cannot but raise the question, 'Is there then any specifically Christian view of the relationships of men and women, anything the Church stands for, or even stands against? Or is it all a matter of economic conditions, social customs and the like, shaping the Church's behaviour willy nilly?'

The answer to that question seems something like this. The relationship of man and woman is not a peripheral interest of human life, it is absolutely fundamental and it is inescapable. Even a decision to lock oneself into a hermit's cell and never see a woman again is a decision in relation to woman—the enjoyment of the good club, the fraternity, the army mess, is the enjoyment of the absence of women. Every man presupposes a woman in having life in him at all, for all have mothers. Nor can woman be abolished, destroyed, removed like a thing, for however much man may try to make her an object, she returns as a subject, she bodies forth the idea of womanliness. If she were dead the very earth itself would suggest her. 'Only a denial of life itself makes it possible to deny the life of the sexes.'[1]

No relationship affecting so profoundly the physical, mental and spiritual life of individuals and of groups, is capable of being reduced to a single verbal principle: *it is expressed in living, not in words*. But 'living' means 'being in the world' as well as being in the Church. Only in very exceptional circumstances does the sphere of the Church include the economic or the whole social life of its members. That may happen in times of persecution, or when a religious community sets sail for a new land and lives as a working unit. But for the most part the sphere of the Church and the sphere of society overlap but are not co-terminous, and relationships between men and women run through both. It is not therefore surprising that there is a considerable, and in highly differentiated cultures a very intricate, interplay of influences between the Church and society.

In so far as it has encouraged its laity to 'learn in the Church and act in the world' the Church itself has helped to make the social pattern of the relation of the sexes which exist in so many countries today. Society is frequently the proper place in which to take action on some abuse against women, to raise their status and to enable them to live the life of persons. For example, public opinion a century ago was affronted by the suffering inflicted on some women by the existing laws of property. If a woman, married to a drunken bully, removed herself to another house to protect herself and her children, not only all her property but all her earnings she was legally bound to hand over to her husband. The action of the Church was not to appoint a few women bishops or moderators to demonstrate its high regard for women, nor to pass resolutions in church bodies. Action was taken in the legal sphere by Christian laymen jointly with humanitarians, to change

[1] Margaret Mead, *Male and Female*.

the civil law. The same was true in the fields of education, health, child welfare, the care of mothers, and many others. Sometimes Churches have as such taken no action, but their laity have acted in society. In other matters Churches, or groups of Christians coming together for the purpose have raised funds, discovered and supported staff and set in motion a new piece of work which has acted as a 'pattern' copied and improved by other bodies and especially by governments with their immensely larger financial resources.

Whichever the method, whether by independent action of Christians or by groups labelled 'church', the effect has been the same: the Church itself tends to be judged by the yardstick it has helped to make. The Churches have made a large contribution to the field of women's education. In many countries convents opened the first girls' school: in others the education of girls (except of the very wealthiest families) was entirely started by Christian missions. One result of success was that women began to compare their treatment in the Church itself with their treatment in church-promoted educational institutions. Far from raising the cry of 'ingratitude' this fact ought to prompt the reflection that this is the process by which the Church's life is renewed: out of its good endeavours arise those who can urge the Church on to other and better endeavours. Nor is this a western phenomenon. Modern education of women is only a hundred years from its tiny beginnings, yet out of it Indian Christian women are seriously and responsibly questioning the attitude taken by Churches towards the position of women. This perhaps needs saying here because unquestionably in every land most Churches are being criticised both by some of their own members and by outsiders for their treatment of women. It is not always easy to distinguish what is a genuinely Christian criticism of the Church, and what criticism is based on the assumption that the Church is a secular institution and ought to act accordingly. Oversensitiveness to criticism leads on the one hand to a tendency in some church organisations to judge their health by efficiency and numbers and to be constantly striving and straining in an effort to justify themselves. In other parts of the Church's life criticism leads to a defensive and fearful attitude, to condemnation out of hand of the whole modern women's movement and unwillingness to make any experiment or move forward.

This attitude is not confined to the clergy, nor to the male sex.

Any Christian attitude to women and to the relations of men and women, works itself out therefore in a continuing intricate dialogue between the Church and society in real life. Theology plays a part in this dialogue, calling the participants back to the sources of their faith in God and His Word, detecting and grappling with non-Christian conceptions, but it is not determinative. It has never been a theological statement of man-woman relationships which has convinced non-Christians that Christianity really has some positive saving message to mankind in its duality of male and female. The power comes from the recognition—in a world which empirically belongs to the male sex—of a phenomenon, the Christian woman. She may be as different as a Quaker, a Salvation Army lassie, a nun, a deaconess or a Christian mother: she has not a heightened feminity nor is she de-feminised, but the category of the feminine is transcended in her by that of the personal: she is a *person* in the true sense of the word and what she portrays is the mind of Christ. Such a woman may be seen only very rarely, but the point is that she is unmistakably a Christian type and she is the product of grace working through a Church always composed of sinners.

Specifically Christian also is the action of certain groups within the Church. If one tries to look at Church history with the question how men and women have got along together, and what they have made of their calling to be in the order of their creation male and female, and by grace a new creature, one cannot fail to be struck by the importance of the small group working at a particular objective. The influence of the Society of Friends both in Europe and in America, always a small body everywhere, is quite incalculable. From their earliest beginning the Friends not only allowed but expected their women members to participate fully in every responsibility (and danger) borne by men. Their earliest annals are full of accounts of the trials of women itinerant preachers, who did the same work as men and suffered cruelly at the hands of mobs, especially in the universities of Oxford and Cambridge. In some places women were the leaders: one of the chief founders of the Dutch Society of Friends was a woman. So great was early enthusiasm that some young couples left their children and went off preaching, but as time went on excesses of ardour abated, and the Friends began to make their homes the growing point of their movement. Men and women became leaders, not only individually in the service of a new-born Society, but also in a relationship between husband and wife based on equal, if differing responsibility and mutual respect, which held far-reaching social consequences. Their earliest schools were all for boys and girls. George Fox, writing at the end of the seventeenth century expressed his concern 'to give women their place and stir them up to take it'. He based his opinions on Scripture, writing in one of his epistles 'Men and women were helpsmeet in the image of God and in righteousness and holiness in the dominion, before they fell; but after the Fall, in the transgression, man was to rule over his wife. But in the restoration of Christ into the image of God in His righteousness and holiness again, in that they are helpsmeet, man and woman (are) as they were before the Fall'. The Friends were the first in the post-Reformation period to show reluctant Churches what women can do and suffer, and although the Society was taunted with being 'a company of mean folk and women', and knew from experience the problem of the woman with the garrulous tongue, it held firm to its principle of equal partnership. The modern missionary movement, which began not as the action of whole Churches, but as the action of groups within most Churches, also raised the status of women. Long before Christian missions were recognised by Protestant Church authorities as anything much more significant than the escapades of well-intentioned hotheads, they were holding forth to the ancient and primitive religions of the East a practical demonstration that Christianity stood for a view of womanhood undreamed of.[1] Soon however they began to affect the Churches at home. While it was being argued what women could (physically) or might (theologically) do in the equable climates of Europe and America, women were performing tasks in disease-ridden swamps and parched plains which put the home Churches to shame for the niggardliness of opportunity they gave to willing hands.

Often it is the small group or movement that teaches the Church:

---

[1] This is not just a missionary opinion. 'It would be difficult to exaggerate the part played by Christian missions in the emancipation of the Indian woman.' This judgment comes from *Modern India and the West*, a survey by the Royal Institute of International Affairs, London.

some of these break radically with historic Christian tradition and Church order. Most these radical groups contain a high proportion of women among their leading spirits. It is often said this is because women are given to extravagances of religious emotion. Be that as it may, one thing that has driven them into these sects has been the feeling that the main denominations have no place for the woman with an urge to preach, prophesy and cure souls.[1] Women take a large part in the leadership of these sects, both at home and in their missionary activity in Asia and Africa, which is spreading fast and never lacks recruits. Since the World Council of Churches' enquiry into women's work covers only the activities of member Churches, this will be the sole reference in this volume to the sects. Looked at from the angle of this survey they are an attempt to give women equal scope outside the historical line of development.

At the other extreme from the sects, the largest Church in Christendom, the Roman Catholic Church also falls outside the scope of this book. Yet its influence on the Churches here dealt with has been enormous. Part of that influence has been indirect. The Roman Catholic Church has shaped the culture of many countries—Spain, Italy, Central and South America—in which Protestants are a minority. In other respects the influence has been more direct, especially in reaction against Roman Catholic practices or abuses. The violent repudiation of mariolatry at the Reformation no doubt had something to do with the intense masculinity of sentiment of most of the Reformers. Certainly the evil influence of the women attached to many of the later medieval popes and prelates, and their deeds of treachery and violence in the pursuit of power, provided the Reformers with ample reason for repudiating the influence of women. Many Catholics felt as strongly as they. The effect of the suppression of the nunneries at the Reformation has probably been exaggerated, for nunneries had unquestionably dwindled in size and influence long years before the Reformation. Many of them had become convenient places for influential men to put their unmarriageable women folk, and in these serious study and arduous devotion and hard work were replaced by a life of trivial actions and never-ending chatter.

[1] 'Probably the largest number of women pastors are in the Pentecostal and Holiness Groups where there seems to be far less sex prejudice.' American report, p. 70.

It would be difficult to argue that either women or the Church were deprived of an institution of great value when the nunneries disappeared.

After the Reformation, women had a very small share in the life of the Church for several centuries. True, the wars of religion left Europe poor, anarchic and unsafe: the conditions were scarcely present for any development of women's activities outside their homes, and from the home once more spiritual revival came. A revival of piety and devotion and a search for personal holiness was one of the nobler features of the Counter-Reformation. Books of devotion were written: the seventeenth century was an age of letter writing and many of the letters which passed between famous spiritual directors and cultured and intelligent women are read today for their spiritual value—and by many who are not Roman Catholics. In the Reformation Churches a revival of the spiritual life took place in a different way and affected far more people. That the Bible should be accessible to Christians in their own language was a first principle with the Reformers. An immediate change took place in public worship, but the invention of printing and its spread throughout Europe made the Bible a book to read, as well as a book to be heard read in church. It became in course of time the book of the Christian home, the *only* book in countless homes, and here women read and studied it. The revival of piety in the Counter-Reformation led fairly speedily to the revival of women's work through the Religious Orders, and Sisters of Mercy were at work among the poor and diseased long before any Protestant counterparts were to be seen.

Once women in the Protestant Churches began to assume responsibilities, appeal to the Bible was often made as the ground for action. Why was not that appeal made two hundred years sooner—as it could have been? The answer seems to be that the Protestant Churches, having repudiated mariolatry, suppressed the nunneries and denounced the influence of women behind the scenes in Church affairs, were afraid of 'Romish practices' and all too ready to see in any new move a denial of a principle of the Reformation. Not until 1848 was any Religious Order for women established in any Church stemming from the Reformation. Many attempts to found educational establishments for women came to an abortive end when they were castigated as 'attempts to revive nunneries'. Most notable was that of Mary Astell. Seeing nothing but triviality and aimlessness in the lives of women around her she wrote, in 1697, *A Serious Plea to the Ladies*. She planned the building in Chelsea, London, of what would have been, had she succeeded, the first Women's Christian College. Several editions of her book were published, and she got the interest of Queen Anne. But the Archbishop of Canterbury would have none of it—she was trying, he said, to revive the nunneries and that was enough to rouse Protestant suspicions against her. The college in Chelsea remained a dream.

From the Reformation to the nineteenth century women had as little share in the life and work of the Church as they have ever had in its long history. Yet it is impossible to take an altogether gloomy view of this period. Here and there were groups like the Society of Friends, experimenting in equality between the sexes; everywhere the Bible was being read in the home. It was a period of quiet growth in spiritual power among ordinary people and it was from them and not from the accredited leaders of the Churches that new life returned to the Church and with that new life a great upsurge of activity among women.

It is a commonplace to say that the nineteenth century was one of sweeping change. A new civilisation of science and the machine grew up within the fabric of the old Christendom and with it came a phenomenal growth of population. Europe trebled her population in the course of the century, and this growing population was always on the move. It moved from the countryside into the towns, seeking work in the new factories and creating the crowded, unplanned cities. It moved also out of Europe across the seas to the New World of North and South America, to the newly discovered Australasian continent, there to make permanent settlements. A smaller but significant part took to the sea as an occupation and immensely enriched their countries by trade.

In all this immense change there was a task awaiting women which it is quite impossible to believe could have been accomplished by religious orders, by small hospitals staffed by nuns, and by religious foundations in education. Something quite new was required. The uprooted populations which filled the cities had to find some new life in community: the new countries were receiving men and women of every European country, language and faith; how were these populations to be integrated? Trade was bringing the West into touch with the ancient religions and civilisations of Asia to a larger extent than ever before, and a new phenomenon presented itself to the western mind, the 'savage' of the Pacific Islands and Africa. How could the Christian conscience, touched by the sense of obligation to evangelise, find the means of doing so, and how could it attack the menace of slavery which, abolished as a traffic in the early years of the century, was found ravaging the villages of Africa wherever that continent was opened up?

It is customary in these days to blacken the religion of the nineteenth century. Let us admit without question that the packed churches contained many who were there for reasons other than the worship of God, that there was much hypocrisy, above all that the Churches of that century never succeeded in making the Gospel a living power in the lives of the new city proletariats. But when this has been said the achievement of the Churches in the nineteenth century was a staggering one. Out of private money—and by no means out of the pockets of the rich alone—buildings were erected where new populations arose. 'A church', which hitherto had meant a building for worship with at most a small vestry or a robing room or a room for the lay leaders of the church to meet in, meant, by the end of the century, a block of buildings with place for large meetings, Sunday Schools and classes, kitchens for the preparation of food and equipment varying from a piano to a gymnasium. Local churches in Europe, America and the British dominions overseas set themselves to educate both young people and adults, to provide for leisure, to be the centres of local community life. They tried to help the poor and the sick, to welcome strangers and cheer the aged, and to do this they built and financed a range of institutions over and above the local church, some of them under Church auspices, some privately run by groups of Christian men and women who got most of their financial support and their personnel from the Churches. The Churches at the same time greatly enlarged their regular ministry and gave them a special training for their work and added to that ministry new types of trained workers. All this took place mainly under the leadership of a vigorous and growing middle-class, filled with liberal and democratic ideals, but it did not stop at the middle classes. If the poorest of the poor

were outside the Church (except as the objects of its charity)
certainly large sections of the lower middle class tradespeople
and the skilled artisans were within it, and large sections of
the new industrial communities which were not in the
inner fellowship of the Church were well within its many
organisations.

Great as was the cost and labour involved in building and
manning these new churches, there was still energy enough to
spare for the thought of the evangelisation of great populations
whose very existence had scarcely dinted Western consciousness
a hundred years before. The work of Christian missions expanded
with great rapidity during the century, not only geographically.
The conception of what was meant by 'missions' expanded also
from the simple preaching of the Gospel by spoken words to the
written word and thence to education, and from the care of the
soul to the care of the whole person through healing and social
work. The number of missionaries grew steadily throughout
the century and to them were added native teachers, pastors,
doctors and nurses. Land was purchased, institutions were
built and equipped, missionaries recruited and supported almost
entirely from the private giving of the Churches of the
West.

How was all this done? The Church drew upon its untapped
resources, its laity and very specially upon the women among
them.

The modern pattern of women's work in the Churches is three-
fold. In making its enquiry into women's work the World
Council of Churches assumed that there were three distinct types
of women's work. The result of the enquiry is to show how
many similarities there are in the women's work of Churches
which differ in faith and very markedly in church order. The
reason for this would seem to be that in all Churches women's
activity was a response of the Church to sweeping social change
which affected all Churches alike.

The three-fold pattern can be very easily described. There are,
first, the great voluntary organisations of women in most of the
Churches. The majority of these movements have branches in
local congregations which are more or less closely connected with
regional and national committees. Secondly, there are the women
who serve the Churches as full-time workers, usually paid and

trained. This is the only part of the three-fold pattern with a long history in the Church. The voluntary organisations of women in the Churches are new, nearly all of them came into being in the last twenty years of the nineteenth century. A hundred years before they not only did not but could not have existed, for their existence depends on a state of society in which it is thought proper for women to leave their own homes and meet in the homes of other women. Until there were the type of buildings which are described above it was not possible for women to meet in any numbers, and until women's education had advanced a certain distance there were not the leaders to draw groups of women together. The Churches did not invent women's organisations, in fact, they came rather late into the field. Women (Christians among them) were banding themselves together for all sorts of causes long before they organised themselves *within* the Church. In 1869 Emily Davies, the founder of Girton College, Cambridge, wrote in a letter to a friend, 'It seems to me that although there is an increasing disposition to give women fair play, there is also some tendency to increasing separation. We have not yet come to it in religion, but with Ladies' Committees, Ladies' Associations, Lectures to Ladies and the rest, one does not quite see why we should not soon have Ladies' Churches and Chapels!' Twenty years later, not 'ladies' churches and chapels', but women's organisations with a large degree of autonomy within the Churches were outgrowing in size of membership every other type of women's co-operation.

The third type of work of women in the Church consists of their growing participation in the management of the affairs of the Churches, local, regional and national. This is the latest part of the three-fold pattern to emerge. Here again the influence of modern ideas at large in secular society, and embodied politically in the conception of a liberal democracy, can be seen at work.

The three-fold pattern is by now well established. It is not entirely fixed, and changes within it are constantly taking place. But women's organisations, though perhaps some are not as vigorous as they were, nor as large, are an accepted feature of church life in all but a small number of Churches. The tendency is towards giving women a larger share in the governance of the Churches. For reasons which will become obvious, the oldest

part of the three-fold pattern is at the present time in most difficulties—difficulties of function, of recruitment and of status
within the Church: few doubt that women have a contribution to
make as full-time servants of the Church, but compared to fifty
years ago there are more, and more difficult, questions about what
that place should be. But even with these reservations, the statement that this pattern is well-established is true, and herein lies a
danger. It is fatally easy to begin attaching value to the existence
of women's organisations and women's work, to fall into the trap
of assuming that every Church ought to have organised work for
women and is a poor sort of Church if it has not, and does not
support workers on the mission field to further the work of that
organisation within the younger Churches. Often this is of the
greatest possible benefit, since both workers and money are so
scarce. Yet it can, and sometimes does, raise questions: there is at
least one Church founded by western missions in which there has
been too much work among women, compared with work among
men, with the result that Christianity is now regarded as a
woman's affair by the men. It is an open question whether
women's work as we know it in the West is the last word on
women in the Church: nor is it clear that its spreading so rapidly
to the younger Churches arises from the needs of those Churches
for just these very things, and not in greater or lesser degree from
the determination of western women that the younger Churches
shall have what they themselves most cherish. A danger lies in the
very virtues of women, their ability to make sacrifices and raise
money and the thorough-going nature of much of their organised
work. Few of them think theologically and few theologians turn
their minds to the enormous work done by women and ask what
it all means in terms of a doctrine of the Church. Yet for countless
women work for and with women is the *only* way open to them
to make their contribution to the life of the Church. The more
vigorous the women's activities in a particular congregation, the
more an organisation, group or fellowship tends to *become* 'the
Church' for the woman who finds there Christian fellowship,
worship and the upbuilding of her faith. Thus there can arise in
practice, although the theory of it is denied, a church within a
church, or a church alongside a church. Women constantly feel
that in spite of what is said in preaching the men are really 'the
Church' and their own participation is derivative from and

dependent on, that of men. The question for the future is how the immense achievement of the work of women for women and with women can be made fruitful in the life of the whole Church. This is not a women's question, it is a Church question. But it is necessary first to attempt to describe in the next four chapters what women's work in and through the Church actually is.

II

THE VOLUNTARY SERVICE OF WOMEN
IN THE CHURCH

THE TERM 'Women's Organisation' is now a familiar one
in most countries and most Churches. It commonly means
an organisation of women within the framework of, or in
close association with, a single denomination, having branches in
local congregations and some sort of headquarters organisation
with a staff.

These organisations are the channel through which many
women give their service to their Churches: they are for many
women that part of the Church which provides them with a real
sense of Christian fellowship and the means whereby they learn
more about their faith and how to live it: they provide the means
whereby thousands of women whose main pre-occupation is with
their homes and families can join with other women to use the
slender margin of their spare time in service for others. What are
these organisations to the Churches? That is a question more
difficult to answer. Very little women's work is a charge on the
Churches, while many women's organisations raise sums of
money which are really enormous and hand them over to the
Church authorities for expenditure. At the local level they often
sustain a large proportion of the burden of maintenance: thus, for
example, of certain women's groups in Canada it is said, 'Because
of the efforts and good management of these (women's) groups
many manses and church buildings are kept in repair.' But it is
not only their material help to the Churches that is valued. When
Archbishop Söderblom described the groups of women in the
local congregations of the Church of Sweden as 'the supporting
beams of the Church' he was not thinking of finance, but of faith
and charity. 'Women's groups or societies carry on more than

fifty per cent. of the work of the Church' says the report from Chile.

Yet here and there a note of uneasiness creeps in. Are the women's organisations sometimes likely to become something of an *imperium in imperio* in the Churches? Is there something a little intimidating in the sight of large concourses of women; something a little dangerous in their resolutions? But these doubts are not loudly expressed either by men or women, partly because all know the immense work done for the Church by women's organisations, partly because no one sees any alternative. But there *are* doubts ranging from the fears of some men of women, often expressed in banter, ridicule or patronising talk, to the theological insight of a minority that the health and *wholeness* of the Church are more important than the vigour of a section of it.

Two interesting facts stand out from the reading of these reports on women's organisations. One is that an immense amount of women's work goes on in the Churches without any organisation at all. Some Churches where there are vigorous and active women would not know what the term 'women's organisation' means. That would be true of most of the Churches of the Orthodox confession. Nearly all Churches which have vigorous women's organisations also have a large number of women who are not members of them, and these are even in the majority; and innumerable small groups of women meet for Bible study or belong to a local fellowship or visit old people without belonging to any known organisation of women. The other is that some of these large organisations are not nearly so highly organised or so powerful as they sound. An imposing name may be served by a full-time staff of only two or three, a central committee may often do no more than advise and, far from having the sting of seeing its advice flouted, may never know whether the advice was taken or not.

It seems abundantly clear from the reports that nearly all the large-scale women's organisations in the Churches today began locally not centrally, and that the creation of central machinery was prompted chiefly by the desire to put the points on the periphery into touch with each other. The marks of local origin are still to be seen in many local branches of large organisations, and these marks are not mere survivals of old customs, for there is an

C

ever-present influence at work making for local differences—the local minister who will or will not have certain things done in his church and who holds certain conscious or unconscious attitudes about women and their place in the Church. There is also the minister's wife, the mainstay of so many local women's organisations in the Churches.

There is a rich and interesting field of research, almost unexplored, waiting for any historical scholar to enter, in the early beginnings of women's work in the opening years of the nineteenth century. The slow awakening of the Christian conscience to the social condition of the poor created by the industrial revolution went on side by side with the awakening of women to responsibilities beyond their immediate family circle. Thus in Germany the first women's groups to be found in the Churches were in the towns where there was an influx of population from the countryside and women began to educate the children in Sunday Schools and to work in the Inner Mission. In the United States 'probably the first women's organisations of any kind were the "cent" or "mite" societies to raise money for missions in the early 1800's. One of the earliest was a Boston one in the very early 1800's, even before the American Board. It was concerned particularly with work for the Indians, which they thought of as "foreign" missions but which we would now consider home missions. A few larger societies were formed in the first half of the nineteenth century, but as the Civil War drew nearer, the struggle over slavery absorbed people's attention and less was done'. In Canada a group of Presbyterian women in the little Province of Prince Edward Island organised a 'Female Society for the Propagation of the Gospel' as early as 1824. In Sweden small groups of women, known as the 'Sewing Guilds', which had their beginnings in spiritual revival, came together in the parishes from an early date to work for the needs of their Church.

With the strong proviso that there always has been and probably always will be a great deal of women's work voluntarily undertaken which falls outside the scope of organisation, it is possible to distinguish two phases of development. In the first, which belongs to the nineteenth century, local women's groups were swept into larger movements as the result of an interest in a cause. In the second phase some of these larger movements have come together into what the Americans call 'over-all organisations' and at the same time have drawn nearer to the headquarters organisation of the Churches.

It will be convenient to group these movements into the main causes which women supported and furthered.

FOREIGN MISSIONS

The swelling tide of interest in foreign missions through the whole of the nineteenth century was the main factor which turned isolated groups of Christian women into a real movement of women throughout the Churches. Men as well as women were caught into this interest, and indeed the planning and organising and the recruitment of missionaries were the task mainly of men. But for women foreign missions had a peculiarly strong appeal, for they met a need in their lives. It is a mistake to suppose that when women meet in groups the only thing they want to do is to discuss their homes and children. They like, as some of them would put it, 'to be taken out of themselves'. In days when travel for pleasure was unknown, when new lands were being opened up, full of strange marvels which there was no camera or cinema to reveal, foreign missions made a powerful appeal to the imagination of countless women whose lives were circumscribed by the trivial round and common task. At the same time they made the appeal which few women can resist—the appeal for practical help in small ways. The odd coins saved from the exiguous budget (less exiguous than the budgets of a generation earlier, for these were days of rising standards of living) could go into the missionary box. Spare moments and spare materials were turned into goods for the poor and needy of whom every missionary could relate. There grew up strong bonds of loyalty and of prayer between the women at home and the women on the mission field. No doubt there were Mrs. Jellybys in this movement, cutting out their red flannel petticoats, and there was scope for the exercise of a sense of power and self-importance, but on the whole the results of this awakened interest were spiritually all to the good. Women began to compare their own comforts and freedoms with the lot of most of those among whom missionaries laboured, and interest passed into sacrifice.

This work for missions obviously demanded some central

organisation. Experiments in forming local missionary societies in direct contact with the foreign field were not successful and died out. Two ways were open to women, either to join their interest to that of the general groups working for missions, or to organise women's mission boards with the special task of sending women abroad and raising the funds for their support. From the earliest days of missionary enterprise, women had gone with their husbands, and some of these returning roused the interest of women at home in the needs of women abroad. Such a one was Mrs. Adoniram Judson, scarcely less famous than her remarkable husband, who went with him to Burma from America in 1815. She had a great influence among women on her return. But in spite of the stories she and her like had to tell, and in spite of the acknowledgement by many men missionaries that work among women was vitally necessary if any semblance of a Christian Church and Christian family life was to grow among the new converts, very few mission boards were prepared to take the terrible hazard of sending single women to the ends of the earth. Probably the London Missionary Society was the first to send a single woman to the mission field, Miss Mary Newell, who went to Malacca in 1827. It was not until about 1870 that any significant number of societies took up the practice. In the meanwhile, a few stalwarts found their own way abroad at their own expense. The women of the Churches, especially in America, took the matter into their own hands and founded special women's missionary societies. The Methodist Female Missionary Society, founded in 1819 in New York, seems to have been the pioneer in this matter, sending Mrs. Ann Wilkins to Liberia in 1837, and supporting her with funds raised by women. Another early Methodist women's society was the Ladies' China Missionary Society organised in Baltimore in 1848. One particularly interesting organisation was an interdenominational society, the Women's Union Missionary Society founded in New York in 1861. Its first missionary had been sent to Burma in that same year, and by 1883 it had sent 43 women to the mission field and found the means for their support.

Foreign missionary work was by no means so readily accepted as an inescapable part of Christian witness a century ago as it is today, and in taking up missionary work as an interest women were often ahead of the main body of opinion in their Churches.

A remarkable example of this is to be seen in the work done by women for missions in the Disciples of Christ (U.S.). In 1874 the Christian Women's Board of Missions was founded in Cincinatti. The Disciples' churches were located mostly in the Middle West, where until recently they had been frontier churches, and some still were. Most of these churches were small and poor and the idea that money should be spent on foreign work when there was so much to be done at home was not the general view. The women planned to work both for home and foreign missions. From the beginning they organised their own work, held property and decided on their own fields of service. With the exception of the Women's Missionary Society of the United Brethren, women's societies employed only women missionaries, but from the first this Disciples' society sent out both men and women, their first missionaries being a married couple sent to Jamaica.

The United States was certainly not the only country in which from an early date women organised for the support of Missionary work. The Scottish Ladies' Association sent the first unmarried woman abroad from that country in 1838, a certain Miss Reed. She was not called a missionary, that title being reserved to men, but was to take charge of work among women under the supervision of the missionaries. The women of other denominations in Scotland sent women abroad in the years following. In Holland the Netherlands Missionary Society was founded in 1797 as the result of an open letter from the London Missionary Society, and a Women's Aid Society assisted this mission from an early date. But it was certainly in America that women created the largest number and variety of groups for the support of foreign missions, and this often with much discouragement and even opposition from their denominational leaders, who had always to be consulted but often gave way only under great pressure and with reservations—unless, as in some cases, they were short of money and glad of help! There seems to be only one example of a Church actually initiating a women's organisation for missionary work, the Protestant Episcopal Church of America, at a late date when most of the fracas about missions and some of the outrage about women's work had died down.

Although the modern trend is towards a single organisation

x   But IPCh — 1873

for women in a single Church, there are still Churches with women's foreign mission committees and still many local congre gations in which a keen missionary group has thought an occasional programme in a larger organisation a doubtfully valuable compensation for the loss of independence. Interest in foreign missions takes a real hold on the minds of many women, in spite of the counter-attractions of other forms of church work.

HOME MISSIONS—EVANGELISM AND SOCIAL SERVICE

It is not easy to give to any other interest leading to the growth of definite movements among women quite the same clearly etched boundaries as can be given to foreign missions.

The conception of 'Home Missions' ties together two important elements, evangelism and what in modern terms is called social service. The early founders of Home Missions would have thought it impossible that the two activities could be separated. To care for the needy and destitute a Christian must give not only bread and shelter but the Gospel, and to evangelise men and women meant to care for their whole lives and persons. They would be profoundly shocked if they could see how the two activities have become separated and often carried out by quite different persons, and alarmed if they knew how many Christians think that both these works should be done by 'experts'. The enthusiasm for foreign missions brought great spiritual benefits to churches and to women's organisations in particular, but there was one danger in this enthusiasm. It was clearly not possible for more than a tiny minority to go abroad as missionaries, while for each woman on the field several hundred were working to support them and praying for their work. All this was excellent unless and until those who stayed at home began to feel that attending a missionary working party and taking the missionary magazine were a substitute for personal evangelism and personal service. 'Home Missions' were in a few respects likely to cause the same difficulty if, for example, the projects were geographically as remote as the foreign mission field or if they were highly technical and only to be conducted by the expert. But with these exceptions Home Missions have offered to Christians the chance for professional worker and volunteer to work together in personal evangelism and personal service.

Amongst the oldest and the greatest of Home Missions is the Inner Mission in Germany. It had its rise in the terrible time of poverty, suffering and moral degeneracy which followed the Napoleonic wars. The Churches were weak and apathetic, but there were men and women in them who were neither. The Inner Mission is usually reckoned to have been founded by one Immanuel Wichern in Hamburg, though his work was preceded by that of other reformers, notably by John Falk, who at Weimar founded one of the earliest reformatories, where he taught trades to boys who had grown up as beggars and criminals in the years of famine. Immanuel Wichern and his mother and sister with a group of friends founded an orphanage outside the city of Hamburg, known as the Rough House. Here boys with histories behind them of living among criminals were taken in to live with the Wicherns in one family. Nothing then was known of casework, of psychology, of the relation of crime to mental deficiency, or the right types of institutions and of persons to effect a reorientation of life. Without this knowledge, but with a great love of God and understanding of boys, Wichern was as successful as any up-to-date social worker; and his boys, having gone through the usual stages of running away and of smashing up the place, received the thanks of the Senate for the work they did in fighting the fire and rescuing the homeless when a great fire swept Hamburg. Within twenty years, twenty more houses were founded by Wichern for boys and girls. The Revolution of 1848 laid bare the condition of the German people, and Wichern felt the urge to do something for the people of Germany and not for Hamburg alone. There were by now many other local reformatories, but Wichern began to take children from other states. More important for the future, he began to train young men who came to him from many parts of Germany and Switzerland for home mission work. They lived with the boys in the homes, giving their time partly to study, partly to being the older brothers of the boys, and partly to work in the farms and workshops which had grown with the houses. This Brotherhood of trained and dedicated men was the heart of the Inner Mission, its members penetrating to every part of Germany.

Here, then, was the framework of a great home mission work, in which men who gave their whole lives to it shared the work with volunteers in orphanages, reformatories, prison work, hospitals and institutions for the physically and mentally afflicted. From the first women were associated in this work, and when the Deaconess movement (see Chapter III) grew to its full strength there were women as well as men to give whole-time service to the Inner Mission. Now the majority of workers in the innumerable societies and undertakings which make up the Inner Mission are women. Soon there was hardly a branch of social and medical work which was not being undertaken by trained men and women and their voluntary supporters. Of the women working now in the Inner Mission the German report says 'they work in so many spheres and are cared for by so many different societies and organisations that we do not possess any information as to numbers, nor could we obtain it without much time and trouble'.

This last remark may be applied with equal truth to every country under review. It is utterly impossible to tell the tale of work being done by trained women with the support of volunteer groups who give both money and time. It covers every imaginable kind of social work and much of it is local and may not even be known to the headquarters group to which the local group is affiliated. Examples of such local work appear in the reports from all countries—house to house visiting, family case work, hostels for young girls coming into the cities, education for home-making among young people, work for refugees, work on the railways, the running of convalescent and rest homes. The number and variety of these local pieces of work is past description and computation. It is interesting to note how a previous generation's concern for orphans and the running of orphanages, though it is not absent from these accounts, is more often than not replaced by a similar concern for the aged. Homes for old people, varying from hostels where they are completely cared for to flatlets where the old people can still have their own possessions and look after themselves unless sick, are among the pieces of service undertaken by single groups of women or by inter-denominational groups in a town. One especially interesting piece of work is a Salvation Army Hostel (London) where women convicted by the courts for child neglect are taken in with their children and taught how to care for their children and how to run a home: follow-up work is an essential part of the success of this scheme.

One of the best-organised pieces of social work undertaken by the women of a Church is that of the Dutch Reformed Church in South Africa. It is worth quoting in full the comment made on it by a leader in a women's organisation of another Church in South Africa, 'While the Dutch Reformed Church has never considered with favour the tendency of the other Churches to give women more responsibility, or to allow them a voice in the highest courts of the Church, they have outstripped other Churches in their work through social service, and in many cases their social workers are supported by the algemene christilike vroue vereeniging (General Women's Christian Union), while homes for the aged and hostels for the lower income group girls were founded under their inspiration or are still supported by them'. The Transvaal South African Women's Federation of the same Church works among the European population, especially the poorer sections of it, and not only does work which is fairly common in women's organisations, but runs institutions for domestic training, health centres in villages, and has a maternity hospital where nurses are trained and work is carried on from it over a wide area. At least one other Church women's organisation in South Africa gives financial support to the social work of the Dutch Reformed Church and it is also subsidised by the Government.

Of all the reports received by the World Council about social work carried on by voluntary women workers, none is more striking than the account sent from Greece of what the women did under the leadership of the Church during the years of Italian and later German occupation, when their country was ravaged by terrible famine. No full account of this work has ever been published, but nothing more than a summary of it is possible here.

There were and are no voluntary movements of women in the Greek Orthodox Church, but there existed before the war a church organisation for charity, known as the General Charitable Fund, founded in 1925. Its central committee under the Archbishopric of Athens consisted of fourteen men and women, and there were committees of women in every parish under the leadership of the priest. In many places this charitable work was closely linked with evangelism, the groups of women who formed the committees organising Biblical teaching and prayer and quite frequently addressing congregations in church at the end of the liturgical service. This organisation was, however, quite insufficient and unsuitable for dealing with the calamity of famine which fell on the Greek people in the autumn of 1941. Archbishop Damaskinos, knowing that this was so, and that the (State) Ministry of Relief and Welfare would—as it subsequently did— prove incapable of rallying the moral force needed in so vast an emergency, made a direct appeal for voluntary help and undertook the leadership himself. The immediate response was 6,500 volunteers, of whom 5,000 were women. The National Organisation of Christian Solidarity was immediately set up, with a strong committee in Athens under the Archbishop, and provincial organisations under the bishops throughout the country. 'Anybody who lived in Greece during the winter of 1941–42 knows the meaning of the word misery. This was not usual poverty: this was absolute destitution, absolute absence of the elementary means of preserving life. This destitution was shared by the greater part of the Greek people and was far from comprising only that section which in normal times constituted the poor. Directly the Archbishop sent out his appeal, women stepped out of this starving and miserable population and volunteered. They worked with all their heart and soul, seeking to relieve the misery around them, forgetting their own equally miserable condition, their own hunger, their worn out shoes and clothing for three whole years.'

The situation with which these volunteers had to grapple defies description. As the Greek army was driven back by the invading Italians, villages were burnt and crops destroyed. Thousands were taken prisoner; others, including some British soldiers, were kept in hiding. The Italians and later the Germans lived off the land without supply lines of their own, and they used famine as a weapon to keep in check a peculiarly independent and courageous people. Hostages were constantly taken from among the population, their families were plunged into destitution and despair. The shooting of hostages took place with increasing frequency, sometimes as many as two hundred at a time being shot without anybody knowing the names of those who were taken. Children wandered the streets and collapsed from hunger, many did not know their family names, or anything about their homes except that 'it had a green door'. Old people were abandoned or died in their homes with nobody to help them.

One of the most striking things about the Organisation of Christian Solidarity is that case work in the homes of the people preceded any setting up of soup kitchens and the like. In all times

of distress countless people will suffer and die in their homes
rather than flock into the streets. From the first these women
volunteers were organised around the parish into what were
called 'annexes' and carried out systematic visitation. The annexes
are described as the eyes of the Organisation. When the International Red Cross arrived to help, they found the organisation
they needed ready to hand and made full use of it. These visiting
women reported all they saw. They knew when the sick needed a
doctor, and doctors and sometimes private clinics were attached
to the annexes. They watched the condition of the children, they
saw that many families needed work, and when the distribution
of clothing began they took the materials to the homes for women
to work on. They were there to help those who lost the heads of
their houses as hostages, and provided for the children while the
women looked for work. And all the time a personal and spiritual
ministry accompanied their work. They found the couples who
were living together without marriage, they had the children
baptised.

In February 1942 the organisation began to open special messes
for feeding children under school age. Within six weeks 28
messes were operating in the Athens area and others in the
Piræus and in other towns. By the end of that year they were
supplying and working 89 messes, from which over twelve million
meals were given out in ten months. By the end of 1943, when full
working with the International Red Cross was established, there
were 197 centres, including shelters for children whose mothers
were working and messes for destitute students. A dozen orphanages were opened, not without very great difficulty, for every
large building was held by the occupying powers and supplies
for furnishing were almost impossible to obtain. The children
taken into them were the most desperate cases: almost all suffered
from famine diseases, many could not eat the food that was offered
to them without sickness. 'They had to be taught to smile' said
those who worked with them. Yet the small size of some of these
orphanages meant that there was family care, and the high degree
of success—only one child died—was due to the devotion given
to them by nurses specially trained to deal with the effects of
famine. In addition the Organisation had 153 children adopted
into Greek families.

The Organisation had a clothing department and a medical

department, through which thousands of inoculations were given, minor operations performed and sick mothers cared for. The difficulties were very great. At first there was help to be had from the better-off sections of the people and they gave generously. Three thousand children were given a meal a day by a better-off family in the early days of the famine. The main funds came from the government, but inflation reduced the value of the grants before they reached the coffers of the Organisation. All money was accounted for with scrupulous care by an audit department. The occupying powers looked on this work with the greatest suspicion because it all helped to keep alive the spirit of the Greek people. Students going to messes were liable to be arrested, but the Organisation overcame this difficulty. Round the messes the women managed to keep alive organisations of Scouts and Girl Guides, (though as organisations these were dissolved and their renewal forbidden) and many of the older boys and girls helped in the service of the needy.

Within the Organisation some groups of women carried out special tasks of very great difficulty. One such group was known as 'the second bureau', simply because it had an office next door to the Archbishop's secretary. Here six women worked. Their main and avowed task was to help the families of those who were prisoners or had been shot as hostages. Actually they assisted many who were resisting the enemy. They were under constant suspicion, and their office was ransacked for proof of complicity in resistance. The work they did in receiving the clothes of the executed and showing them to the crowds of women who had relations in prison and feared the worst, was harrowing in the extreme.

The Organisation worked as vigorously in some provincial towns as it did in Athens itself, assisting more than 1,000 families in other parts of Greece. A notable report comes from the town of Volo in Thessaly. Here the same system of relief was followed and again the same co-operation with the Red Cross took place. Often the women were in close touch with the guerillas and took letters to and from them. They were patriots—but they were also Christians, and out of their supplies they issued 40,000 meals to Italian prisoners of war before they went home. This town established something in the nature of a 'mother house' for its work, called 'the Christian Home'. This was not only or even chiefly an administration centre, it was a centre of evangelism. Here there were lectures and discussions on religious subjects, many of them given by women, a club of six hundred mothers and no less than fifteen study, Bible and catechetical groups through which the faith was made known. It also had two branch houses in smaller towns. This work continued after the end of the war.

This long account from Greece should not be taken to mean that this is the only country in which Christian women have done valiant social work, especially during the emergency of the war. The French report contains an account of similar work, though on a very small scale, done among refugees by women in Grenoble. Wherever there has been distress in recent years, arising out of the war, women have helped to allay it. Many of them worked tirelessly in the refugee camps in India during the riots which followed the partition of the country: work has been done in refugee camps in Germany and in Palestine. Women who were not forced to face such calamities on their doorsteps raised funds and made and sent goods for those whose misery they had never seen—a task which demands imagination. This work has been done ceaselessly in the United States, the British Commonwealth, Switzerland and Sweden. Nevertheless the story of the work done by women in Greece is not only an honourable one in itself, it also shows a pattern of women's work which is not known in other parts of the world. There are similar accounts of women of the Orthodox Churches in Egypt doing active social work under the leadership of their bishops and priests. It is an immense strengthening to evangelism when good social work is known by those who receive it to be done by and in the name of the Church. Nor does one gather the impression that women were deprived of leadership because the bishop was the organisational head, for they held posts of responsibility and acted as chairmen of various sections of the work. No doubt there were places where if the priest was slack the whole work lagged. There were no existing women's organisations to take the lead, but the great advantage of this was that there were no committees and secretaries to steer round or work through. The whole organisation was fashioned to fit the circumstances and dissolved when they had passed. The Church was thus able to call upon a far larger number of women, including many who were not the sort to be attracted by the usual kind of all-women's voluntary organisation. Men and women worked together in this task—the main reason why there were not more men was that so many were prisoners or had fled to the Middle East to continue fighting.

One more example may be given of voluntary social service, that of the Railway Mission in Germany. This is a part of the Inner Mission work, and works in association with the Roman Catholic Railway Mission. It grew up 50 years ago as an offshoot of the work of the Girls' Friendly Society, its aim being to protect young girls travelling, to give shelter to those who were stranded and advice to any in difficulty. The offices and canteens of the Railway Mission are to be seen on all the main railway stations in Germany today, staffed by trained paid helpers and by local volunteers. Like every other type of social work it was taken over by the Nazis as part of their policy for shutting the Church out of ordinary life as much as possible. At the end of the war when Germany was filled with refugees the Railway Missions turned air raid shelters into accommodation and provided food as far as possible. Materials and helpers came through the *Hilfswerk*, the parishes and various women's groups in the Churches. As the flood of refugees abated the Railway Mission gradually returned to their usual work of caring for all travellers in distress.

Like the foreign mission interest, the home mission interest has led to definite movements or organisations with headquarters, staff and literature. In Scotland the women of the Church took an active interest in the poverty-stricken condition of the Highlands, as early as 1845. In England interest centred on church extension, and a tremendous work was done to provide churches and schools for a population growing at an unprecedented rate, while groups of women interested themselves in a large range of social service not officially linked with the Churches. In the United States, women's groups for Home Missions were first organised in the late '60's of the last century. These were concerned with Indians sometimes, but much more with the Frontier, with providing churches and pastors in new areas in the West. Sometimes small groups of church members went from the East to help form the nucleus of a new congregation: more often it was the raising of money for building and the training and sending of parsons which was necessary. This work was the work of the Church as such. Although the money might be raised by special organisations, the result of spending it was new churches, which became a part of the body of the Church and not institutions attached to the society which had raised the funds to build them. Home missionary organisations of women in the United States, therefore, tended always to swing nearer to the Church, either to become part of the general board of the Church or to work in close association with it. Foreign missionary boards tended also to emphasise that their work was an integral and essential part of the work of the Church and they also moved closer both to Home Mission boards and to the governing bodies of the denominations.

THE MODERN OVER-ALL WOMEN'S ORGANISATION

The over-all type of women's organisation springs from the amalgamation of groups concerned with foreign missions and groups concerned with home missionary interests into single organisations, and from the movement to bring both closer to the main life of the Church. What follows does not apply to the situation in the countries of Europe except Great Britain. These European countries have followed a different line of development which will be dealt with later.

The most powerful movement towards amalgamation has taken place in the United States. 'The American trend' says the American report, 'is toward an inclusive women's organisation that undertakes to bring into its work all the varied types of activities carried on by women's groups . . . three denominations have carried this out through all or nearly all their women's organisations: the Presbyterian Church in the United States, the Southern Baptist Convention and the Methodist Church. (These are among the largest Churches in the United States.) The national women's missionary societies of the Methodist Church disappeared into this overhead women's organisation when the merger between three Methodist Churches of the United States took place in 1940. At the same time the 1940 General Conference gave instructions to local churches that local units of former organisations were to come together into a single Women's Society of Christian Service. 'This' the report continues, 'is now nearly complete.' Although the Methodist Church has gone further than any other Church in the United States to bring about a unification of missionary and other groups both in the local churches and at

headquarters, other Churches have gone a long way towards this
goal. In most other Churches it seems that about half their local
congregations have achieved either a single women's organisation
in a single church, combining the old 'Missionary Groups' and
'Ladies Aids', or a method of federating women's groups to
insure that overlapping is reduced to the minimum. It ought to be
added that these omnibus women's organisations are not the end
of smaller groups within a local church, and in any large congregation there are likely to be small groups, based on age or interest,
which form a part of the women's organisation.

The strong move towards centralisation in the United States
is likely to be misunderstood elsewhere, especially in countries
where centralisation is thought to be the immediate destruction
of local initiative. The reason for the growth of strong central
organisations in American church life is almost certainly to be
found in the size of the country. It is a most remarkable thing
that from the Atlantic to the Pacific, from the Canadian border to
the Gulf of Mexico the denominations preserve in their members
a sense of belonging to a body with a common life and common
purposes. Only the centre can bring the points on so wide-flung a
circumference into touch with each other. Printing and paper and
correspondence take the place of frequent meeting and especially
help to bring to isolated rural groups of women both a sense that
they belong to a great Church and also a knowledge of the needs
and problems of others which they would never gain if left to
isolated action.

A somewhat similar trend toward centralisation is to be seen
in Canada, Australia, South Africa, New Zealand and Great
Britain. The same pattern is beginning to emerge in countries
where Churches have been founded by the missionary activity of
the Churches mentioned here. In Australia there are nation-wide
women's church organisations. In Canada most of the Churches
have women's organisations which embrace the whole country,
though the Baptist women's organisation is organised on the
basis of six provinces. Nearly all these centralised organisations
have been created in the last twenty years, drawing into them
existing bodies and usually defining in their new constitutions
both their aims and their relationship to the Churches.

Some of these new central organisations keep the word 'missionary' in their title, but even if they do they define their aims in

broader terms. Others are called Auxiliaries—such as the Women's Auxiliary of the Episcopal Church (U.S.A.), which almost seems to imply that women are auxiliary to the Church, not an integral part of it. Most of them define their purpose in some such terms as these 'To unite the women of the Church in fellowship and service', explaining what they mean by these terms and adding to them in many cases 'study' or 'education' as a further object. What characterised the early movements of women was their extrovert attitude. They came together to learn and to act, and to pray about what they felt called to do. Any idea that their group was the place where they discovered what the Christian faith was scarcely occurred to them. The church itself was the place in which to learn the faith and there were Bible study groups for those who wanted them. But much has happened since those days. The Christian faith and especially the knowledge of the Bible are not taught in the home as they used to be: the faith is under fire from secular critics, and Christian believers are not unaffected by the general bewilderment abroad in society. The Christian ethic is also under challenge, especially Christian teaching about marriage. It cannot be assumed that a group of church women need no teaching: they are often only too well aware that they do. So there has been a shift from an almost wholly extrovert attitude to one which is much more concerned with the needs of the members of the group themselves in learning and practising the faith, in Christian home-making and in learning what the Church is and what their place is in it.

There is no doubt that at the centre all this amalgamation has made for increased efficiency and has cut out much overlapping. It is too early yet to say what the permanent effects are going to be in the local congregations, but one thing is already clear. Report after report speaks of a crisis in leadership; of the shortage of women to take local leadership; of the numbers of women who do not stay in office more than a year; of the social causes of this shortage in lack of domestic help and post-war complications in housekeeping; and of the diffidence of women who have had no opportunity or experience. But part of the difficulty lies in the enlargement of the task which is laid on the shoulders of local leaders. It is one thing to lead a missionary working party with a monthly speaker, quite another thing to lead a large group composed of a considerable number of all the women of the

D

church of different ages, interests and education, a group which is much less a working party and much more a microcosm of the Church itself, in which the elements of worship, teaching, study, practical effort, social recreation and a good deal of pastoral care of the members have to find a place. This is too much for most women. It has to be the work of a committee and that introduces new difficulties for the leader. Meanwhile the world over one class is being taxed beyond its strength by the demand for local leadership—the ministers' wives who as a class have suffered a great decline in their standard of living. The wonder is, not that many movements are short of local and even national leaders, but that such a tremendous number of movements do thrive and draw out from unexpected people qualities of leadership which the Church as a whole is not tapping.

Two main concerns are therefore exercising nearly all the head-quarters staffs of women's movements, the training of leaders and speakers for local groups and the preparation of printed pro-grammes for six months' or a year's meetings which give the leader ideas which she can embody in her own programme, or even detailed suggestions for meetings which she only has to carry out. Many organisations have training courses for leaders and speakers, sometimes lasting two or three days. These are often on a regional basis. They frequently combine the more or less technical questions of how to address a meeting, run a com-mittee, organise a branch, with worship and addresses designed to help the worker to go back to her job encouraged and refreshed in spirit. Various means are devised to meet the expenses of those who come to these courses, and many women speak with en-thusiasm of the hospitality given in the homes of members to any visiting group. Retreats, quiet days and single day conferences are all organised with success.

Two or three reports comment on the universal complaint that women have no time for the work of leadership in the Church. The Canadian report comments on the immense amount of time spent by women on war work through voluntary organisations, and remarks that the Churches missed a golden opportunity when they failed at the end of the war to draw this leadership into the service of the women's organisations in the Church. Canadian women's organisations are now making a tremendous drive to secure and train leaders. Yet another cause of shortage is to be seen in another report. One woman so completely carried an organisation on her shoulders that nobody else dared to be chosen as her successor and court comparison! Not many women know how to delegate.

The working out of programmes varies very much. A common American practice is to draw up a programme at headquarters and then to remit to a single person the writing of a study book or pamphlet suitable for use in a large number of groups. Other organisations publish magazines for workers in which the successful experiments of some groups are handed on to others. Such papers often contain suggestions for reading by leaders and draw attention to public events which ought to be talked about in the local group. These magazines, or in some cases typewritten notes, for leaders and workers in the groups, are distinct from the magazines for members which very many women's organisations now publish.

The greatest benefit from set programmes is derived in remote country districts where often the women's group is the liveliest part of a church, and has comparatively heavy responsibilities, with very small resources in leadership and even less in visiting speakers. Town churches with more activities going on within them often do not take the central programme, but work on projects more closely aligned to what the Church as a whole is doing.

Even organisations which are not greatly in favour of organising programmes from the centre get so many requests for ideas that they are compelled to take some sort of action. The dangers of the programme system are fairly obvious, not only that local initiative may lapse, but that it opens the possibility for a small group with particular views to put their ideas over on many thousands of women, especially if the shaping of programmes is in the hands of a small group of headquarters staff. It is very easy too for such a group to work itself out of ideas, and there is evidence that women in positions of responsibility at the head of women's organisations are middle-aged when they arrive at these positions and tend to stay there a long time.

A further problem of leadership in women's organisations is the type of woman who tends to be selected for the presidency and committee membership and, more important, for full time service. Women's organisations very rarely look for a woman with theological qualifications. Most of their headquarters staffs and leaders are women who have served the movement well locally and regionally, with gifts of administration, handling committees and public speaking. Most of them are women of good education, but few have had experience of other worlds than that of women's organisations in the Church. There is almost everywhere a danger of women's organisations being a world of their own with too little contact with the outside world, and with secular women's groups. It is useless to suggest that this lack could be met by the appointment of more theologically trained women. What is needed is that some of these great movements with money to command and a great influence in the Church and potentially, if not actually, a really powerful influence to wield in the world outside the Churches, should take a leaf out of the book of the universities, who often in choosing men and women for important positions look outside the academic world and go for a wide experience, imagination and the will to change things. There is a place, too, in the staffs of these movements for more theologically trained women to help to lift the religious teaching out of the rut into which women so easily fall—a too exclusive preoccupation with religion as personal pietism.

OTHER INTERESTS CONTRIBUTING TO THE OVER-ALL ORGANISATION

(a) *Christian marriage and the family.*

Home, family and the training of children are predominating interests in the lives of most women, and time is devoted to them in most modern women's movements in the Church. In some organisations there may be little more done than an occasional lecture or discussion, but some women's organisations do much more. Some of the Protestant Women's Societies in Switzerland which have recently formed an inter-cantonal Federation have advice centres for mothers and run courses in sewing, cooking nd infant management.

One piece of church work directed to the needs of mothers alone is the *Mütterdienst* (mother service) within the German Evangelical Church. In the early 'thirties unemployment in Germany reached astronomic figures: thousands of young people reached manhood without knowing what it was to do a single day's work: families were left utterly destitute. The despair which invaded the heart of the whole nation was the mainstream in the tide that carried Hitler to power. Perhaps the chief sufferers in this misery were the mothers, whose distress was not only for themselves but for the sight of their children's suffering, and which was so often hidden. In Bavaria a small group of women were determined to help. They acquired first one and then several more houses where exhausted mothers could come to be nursed back to health. One of the great features of this work was the emphasis on beauty and on joy. In times of dire necessity it is the beautiful things that go out of life. Nothing can be kept which is not sheer necessity and with beauty the power of recuperation disappears, and joy with it. So these houses were chosen for their lovely surroundings and furnished in good taste, and here for a fortnight or so a mother could be surrounded with care and with little luxuries and helped to recover her will to go on, and given the spiritual strength in which to do so. The work is financed with gifts and by the sale of work and especially of a delightful calendar from its own publishing house, now famous all over Germany. It had a surprising escape from being taken over bodily by the Nazis, and though its work was reduced it never came entirely to a standstill. The centre of the work in Bavaria has also become a centre for the organisation of groups working for mothers in the parishes, often under the guidance of the pastor's wife. It has also been the inspiration for similar work now being undertaken by the Evangelische Reichsfrauenhilfe in other parts of Germany.

There is only one example to be found in the reports of the interest in home and family providing the cause around which a whole denominational movement of women has crystalised. This is the Mothers' Union in the Church of England. This is an Anglican movement with some half a million members. Its three objects are 'To uphold the sanctity of marriage. To awaken in all Mothers a sense of their responsibility in the training of their boys and girls. To organise in every place a band of mothers who will unite in prayer and seek by their own example to lead their families in purity and holiness of life.' The Mothers' Union began in a small village where Mary Sumner, the wife of a country parson, called on some of the women of the village and invited them to meet in her house. So overcome was she afterwards by the novelty of her request and by shyness, that on the appointed day she shut herself in her bedroom and caused her husband to go round the village making her excuses. Later, chiding herself for her faithlessness she repeated her invitation, and the Mothers' Union was born, in 1876. Twenty years later it was a nation-wide movement with a constitution governing membership and activities. It has always been inflexibly opposed to divorce. Although it is open only to married women, with an associate membership for unmarried women, the Mothers' Union is the only women's organisation of the Anglican Church in England and in many dioceses overseas, except for the Girls' Friendly Society. Of the two the Mothers' Union comes nearer to performing the functions of the typical 'overall' women's organisation in the parish, where a branch may only be started with the permission of the minister. A Mothers' Union Branch often performs in a parish the same work as is done in other Churches by a Women's Auxiliary or Ladies' Aid. The missionary interest has been canalised in the Mothers' Union in an interesting way, for the Mothers' Union supports trained workers in a number of overseas dioceses. They promote work among women on Mothers' Union lines— thus, for example, the Mothers' Union in New Zealand supports a mothercraft worker in the Solomon Islands, while from Headquarters in London 32 workers are supported in most of the colonial dioceses of the British Empire, to work under the bishops in close touch with any Anglican missionary society in the field.

It may well be asked why only one women's movement has grown out of concern with marriage and family while foreign missions have given rise to so many. The answer may well be that at the time when foreign missions and home missions were calling forth so much effort from women, not much concern was being expressed in the Churches about the family. It was an age of strong parental discipline and strict religious teaching in the homes of most church-going people. There was little if any anxiety expressed about a possible decay in Christian family living. Those who possessed it took it for granted and did what they could, according to their lights, to provide it for children without homes, though they often failed to transfer to the orphanages they built the affection which so often tempered discipline within the family. All this has radically changed. Christian parents no longer feel so confident that they know exactly how to bring up children and shape their own marriages on a Christian pattern. The trouncing which the psychologists have given to the nineteenth century certainties leaves many parents perplexed, for the swing from authority to individualism has not solved the new problems it has created. The loosening of marriage ties in most modern communities has compelled the Churches to examine their principles and look to the instruction and help they give to their members.

It is by now clearly recognised that the right time to give Christian teaching about marriage is before marriage, and Christian youth movements play an important part in providing a place where Christian teaching about marriage can be given and discussed. The younger generation is not prepared to say that the making of a Christian home is the exclusive responsibility and privilege of the woman, and younger men and women are prepared to discuss these matters happily in the atmosphere of a good mixed club. This causes many young women to ask why, at the age of twenty-five or so the Churches seem to expect young women to leave their mixed clubs and join an organisation exclusively for women. In one sense their protest is wise. The natural interests of the woman are much more closely identified with the preservation of the family than the natural interests of the man, and it is important that the Churches should make it clear that their teaching about marriage is not just a reinforcement of the natural disposition of the majority of women. When the only things that are said or done about marriage and the family are said and done in the women's groups in the Church, then it does look as though tacitly if not explicit the Church assumes that the responsibility for Christian marriage and homes is 'a woman's affair'. But once a joint responsibility of men and women for upholding Christian marriage has been recognised there is clearly a place for an all-women's discussion of the care of children, for the day to day upbringing of children does fall inescapably to the mother in the home.

Nowhere is it so urgent that the witness of the Christian home should be upheld as in countries where the Church is newly planted in a pagan environment. This is a subject to which the Christian Councils both of India and of China have given attention. The National Christian Council of China found, when a survey was made of country churches, that in congregations with an average membership of fifty, the number of homes in which both partners were Christians was five, and in several city churches (where the membership is large enough for marriages to take place within a congregation) only ten per cent. of the members belonged to homes where both partners were Christians. The Council thought that, although the Christian Home movement in China had done a notable work in improving Christian homes, the basic trouble was that there were too few Christian homes. In many cases the number of children in Sunday Schools was only half that of the total number of members in the church, and this was because in homes where only one parent was a Christian the children often did not receive a Christian education. Unless this was remedied the Christian Church would be bound to die out (unless of course it could make good its losses by evangelism, though this could hardly be regarded as a satisfactory remedy). The report sees the cause of the situation partly in the lack of correlation between the men's and the women's sides of mission work which has prevented sufficient attention being given to building families as opposed to converting individuals. It speaks of the great popularity of clubs for young married couples in churches which had established them. Another difficulty mentioned in a different report from China is the employment of young married women among the educated classes: their services to a society with far too few trained teachers, doctors, nurses and other skilled persons were very obvious, but their employment often meant that the care of the home and the children fell too much into the hands of the grandmothers who thought in the old ways, with the result that just those families which ought to be working out new patterns of Christian family living were failing to do so.

The Christian Home movement in China had in its service an American missionary who improvised all kinds of means for teaching simple people—both men and women—the elements of Christian home making, using visual aids, exhibitions and drama. When Shanghai fell to the communists she was out of the country and re-entry was forbidden. With support from the International Missionary Council she has been able to make a prolonged stay both in Indonesia and in Japan and her expert advice has contributed to the building of Christian Home movements in these countries.

The National Christian Council of India has a Christian Home Committee—an all-women's committee. It runs a periodical, 'The Christian Home'. Regional committees help in the organisation of all kinds of local festivals and conferences on the Christian home. These are popular with young people, and lectures, drama and every available medium are used for teaching on sex, home management, health, temperance, religious education and a great variety of subjects.

'Those who live in large Christian communities are apt to forget,' writes an Indian woman in the report from her country, 'the loneliness of the Christian family in a dominantly non-Christian environment,' and she goes on to describe the Women's Conventions organised by the women of the Methodist District of Hyderabad. Young women from the villages are coming forward in increasing numbers to these gatherings in their own villages and 'take it in turns to conduct the weekly women's meetings and at the daily prayer meetings women tell the stories, read the Bible and lead the congregation in prayer'. An account is given in the Belgian Congo of women being brought together for conferences—'a new venture in the missions where it is being tried, but welcomed by the women', and another report from Africa speaks of similar gatherings 'with a festival air' about them. It is surprising that such meetings can be held, in view of the heavy burdens which fall on the backs of women, 'the majority still do the manual labour of the gardens, the fishing and the harvesting. Men fell the forest trees and do the main clearing: women burn the ground, dig, plant, reap and carry in the food. That they have always done. Now they do that and more, for much of the cocoa that is loaded on steamers has been carried on the backs of women' (Cameroons). Work for truly Christian marriages and home life is very difficult, 'because a great many of the strongest old heathen customs centre around the home and the life cycle of the person. It is in a great measure the wife and mother who must break with these and if she has a heathen mother (as so many of them do) she will find much opposition and even persecution'. Yet the women do come together both in their villages and occasionally to larger centres where travel is possible. In spite of hard work and a long tradition of inferiority to men, women even in the remote parts of Nigeria, the Cameroons and Congo are beginning to have a little money of their own as they sell the produce of their gardens. One report comments that although the men say that the women have nothing they usually know where a little money can be raised for church purposes when it is needed.

Further East than the Western seaboard from which the reports quoted above came there is an interesting women's movement in Bechuanaland and Southern Rhodesia, the result of thirty years of work by a woman missionary. This is a uniformed movement of women called the 'Red Blouse' movement. It has about three hundred branches and some six thousand members. One of the main objects is to teach women the principles of Christian home life and this among tribes which have been polygamous for untold ages, and among whom an unmarried woman of chaste habits is a rarity. The movement exercises discipline over its members who may be deprived of their uniform if they fall from the required standard, and it also does a good deal of training of leaders, bringing them in from their villages to regional Bible schools, for which the women themselves pay by the sale of their eggs, chickens and handwork. Other mission Churches encourage similar movements among women, several of which are also uniformed and disciplined movements.

It is often said in Churches in the West that the woman in her home finds it less of a struggle to try to live up to the Christian teaching she receives than the man in business. It is never looked on as a really difficult and even dangerous form of Christian witness. One of the most salutary reminders which comes out of these reports is that in very many countries the woman who tries to make her home a Christian home is undertaking a dangerous form of witness. She is not only running the risk of the disapproval of husband and mother-in-law: she is setting up in her home a little cell of a movement which threatens to destroy the traditional hallowed social customs of her neighbours and her people. Just as the early Christians who refused to eat meat sacrificed to idols were rightly seen by their contemporaries to be well on the road to destroying the old society, so the women in their homes and in their Christian movements are pitting their strength, faith and powers of endurance against the society in which they live. It is they who have to discover the difficult grace of loving their neighbours and repudiating what they stand for. This reminder comes from all sorts of different situations—from the little tiny groups of women in primitive tribes, from Christian communities in the midst of Islam, and from Protestant women in South America. An Argentina woman describes in these words the task which Christian women have to perform (what she says is amply borne out by reports from all other South American countries where the low status of women, and the prevalence of the double moral standard as between men and women is constantly commented upon as the toughest problem that women have to face): 'The Spaniards came as "conquistadores", conquerors. The men came alone, leaving their families in Europe. Pretty soon they broke family ties and took native women as wives. Their homes were never normally established and the very reverence of human personality was unknown to them. Women had a very low place among such people. It has been the challenge and the task of the Protestant movement in these countries to place women in a different rank, not only in the Church but in society, and through the direct work of the Church as well as through education a new day opened for women.'

(b) *The woman at work*

One of the most notable facts in the census statistics wherever they have been taken since the war is the great increase in the number of women who are in gainful employment. There is a great army of working women, and these include not only young women who are working before marriage, but a higher proportion of widows and women living apart from their husbands. The most significant change is in the number of married women who are employed either in full-time or in part-time work. Even in countries with a strong tradition that a father should provide for his daughter until he hands her over to the care of a husband there has been a remarkable change. Thus in India 'the upheaval of the war and still more of the riots in which so many lost lives and property, have made many Indian fathers feel that they would not be serving their daughters' best interests if they failed to provide them with the training and the opportunity to earn their own livings'.

Women therefore are workers—some for all their lives and most for a part. This means not only that they cannot attend meetings at hours fixed to suit the housewife, but also that they have problems and interests different from those of the woman in the home. The Y.W.C.A. has been the main Christian agency working among younger women at work, and many older women, too, find themselves more at home in its atmosphere than in that of the average women's movement within the denominations. There is hardly a report other than that from the United States which indicates that hard thinking has been given to this important subject, though, as always, absence of information may not necessarily mean that nothing has been done. The American report very well summarizes some of the problems which have been met and in some cases overcome when an effort has been made to meet the special needs in the Church of the woman who goes out to work.

'Some of our Protestant Churches are beginning to realise that the common phrase, "The women will work in the Church anyway" does not apply to the employed woman unless there is a place where she *can* work in the time she has available. The Presbyterian Church in the United States with some 42,500 women in 1,346 business women's circles in 1946–1947 probably has the highest proportion in such organisations of any denomination. The Methodist Service Guild has the largest *number* of employed women in its membership, 3,300 units and over 70,000 members, but that is a relatively small proportion of the employed women in the Methodist Church.

'A few denominations prepare programme materials for "evening groups" often assuming that *all* women who are tied down during the day, whether by family responsibilities or jobs, will wish to work together. At that point there is sharp division of opinion. Some of the most experienced observers question the wisdom of this plan. It is difficult enough, they say, to plan programmes that will interest both the school teacher and the telephone operator or department store clerk, to say nothing of the factory workers, without adding those whose primary interest is in their home and babies. One group or the other is likely to lose interest. Some denominations assume that the "evening groups" will use the same programmes as the day-time groups. Some national women's denominational organisations have seemed to assume that they have little or no responsibility for promoting such groups. Too often, also, the "regular" women's organisations take a patronising attitude toward the employed women, putting on programmes *for* them in making which they have no part, or seeming in other ways to indicate that they are on a lower scale in the organisation "hierarchy". Still another problem is to keep one age group from dominating the others—whether it be the middle-aged women or the younger ones not long out of school or college. Unfortunately, the result all too often is either that there are no activities for employed women or that they tend to become clubs with little direct relationship to the Church, except the fact that they meet in it. Apparently few people, whether church leaders or employed women, have given much serious thought to the question whether there are special types of activities which such women might well render instead of the "chores" that seem usually to be expected of them if they do anything at all in the church.'

(c) *Evangelism*

The average over-all women's organisation which figures in these reports shows a remarkable contrast between the energy expended in social service and on mission support and the paucity of evangelism. It ought perhaps to be underlined that the standpoint of this book is not that evangelism is the proper task of Christians while social service is an addition to, but not an essential part of, their witness. The two belong together. But there is evidence in the reports that some women, including some who have thrown themselves with tremendous energy into work for the Red Cross Society, and for the Red Crescent Society in Mohammedan lands, are asking what difference there is between the Christian and the person of goodwill who does not accept the faith. Some are very glad of the opportunities brought to them by the war and by post-war needs of meeting non-Christians in an easy and natural way. They are conscious that it is all too easy for Christians to live in little huddles together and get out of touch with others and forget how they think. Contact and understanding are unquestionably a prerequisite of evangelism. But the will and the power to evangelise seem to be lacking, and it is scarcely fair to fasten on the women's organisations what is a failure of the Churches as a whole. Indeed, it is fairly clear that in many places the women's organisations are doing more than their Churches to present the Gospel to those who are not Christians in any active sense, or

even nominally, but this is happening in informal ways, sometimes only very loosely connected with the women's organisation.
The Mothers' Union has some two thousand groups known as
Open Groups (i.e. groups in which the conditions of membership
of the Mothers' Union itself are not enforced) and Young Wives'
groups, meeting in the homes of Mothers' Union members. The
Methodist report from the Argentine mentions that they found
themselves with too many branches whose membership was of
elderly women, and have therefore started young wives' groups.
Other reports hint at efforts to bring women together in small
groups meeting in homes, especially in the suburbs of great cities
where women often suffer acutely from loneliness. It is among
young mothers that the Churches have one of their greatest
opportunities today. Although on the face of it almost everything
seems to be done by public health authorities with their clinics and
advice bureaus in which medical and psychological advice are
readily given, what the young mother really craves is the fellowship of amateurs. If the advice she is given fails to meet her child's
needs she is a prey to all sorts of doubts. Is her child abnormal and
is she a failure worse than all others? The group meeting in
another home gives her the companionship she does not know
how to find and the Christian group can often supply her spiritual
needs, for she has her ideals for her child, she wants to do her best
and she knows that the problems between her and her child
cannot be evaluated in terms of vitamins and repressions: they
are problems of relationship and of life.

To turn from the reports from the West to those coming from
Churches planted by missionary activity is to move into a wholly
different atmosphere in this matter of evangelism. Instead of
finding that evangelism is a subject which nags at the conscience
and rebukes the Christian with the thought of what has been left
undone, one finds over and over again that evangelism is accepted
as the first and most joyful of Christian duties. Even those who
are babes in the faith are eager to share what little they have. It
is this inner spirit of joy in the Gospel that makes the difference.
In older established congregations in India, for example, the
eagerness flags and there are women who are heard to say that
evangelism is the business of the Missions with their paid agents
and not of the Church. But wherever there is a transfer of full
authority to the Church from the Mission there tends to be a

revival of this simple enthusiasm and it is harnessed to the best that the older Churches can give—the knowledge of how to organise and how to train. Quite simply Churches and women's movements in the midst of non-Christian cultures know that across their life is written 'evangelise or perish'. That is the fate of all Churches everywhere, the difference being that some do not know it.

The simplest form of evangelism and the one which appears most often in the reports is house to house visitation. This sounds an easy matter, but in countries where it is not customary for women to enter the houses of others it is not simple at all. A non-Christian environment does offer many opportunities which are lacking in the more sophisticated West. Many women long to learn to read and the Christian visitor who can teach a woman her letters is often welcome on that score alone. The Laubach method, perfected by one man and adaptable to almost any language enables a woman who can only just read herself to teach her neighbour: the book read is almost always a gospel and the teaching of its message goes naturally with learning to read. Most often the work done by women in a voluntary way links on to what is done by a trained worker, thus there are often voluntary groups of women helpers who are attached to a mission hospital or child welfare clinic and visit the patients in their homes and the mothers of new-born children, and encourage them to come to the services. But the reports contain accounts of evangelistic work done by women in Churches which have only been established for two or three generations; this is much more systematic and calls for courage, organising ability and hard cash, as well as for great skill in avoiding the snares which organisation creates in countries where there are very few leaders. The Korean report[1] contains a warning note, 'There are now too many committees. Too many of the few trained workers give more time to planning work than they give to actual work.'

One example of organised evangelism comes from Burma. There are strongly rooted women's movements established more than fifty years in some of the churches of Burma, each language group of Burmese, Kachin and Karen, having its own organisation but being linked to the others in a larger Society. 'Because they were formed on the pattern of the Women's Mission Circles in the

[1] Written before the war in Korea.

Home Churches these societies have a strongly missionary interest, and have indeed often been referred to as 'Women's Missionary Societies.' The Burmese Baptist Women's Society supports five women in full-time evangelistic work, and the Karen Society sends out both 'home' and 'foreign' missionaries, the home missionaries working in Lower Burma and the foreign missionaries in the wild hill country bordering on Siam. The women's movements send, and support, evangelists to these remote and rugged valleys. All the work of organisation is done by the women themselves on a voluntary basis. Similar work is done by the Methodist women's organisations.

India has her own Missionary Society, the National Missionary Society, and this is keenly supported by women's groups in many different churches. The Indian missionaries of this society work for the most part in remote rural areas, and they are involved in the same uprooting from their own language and culture and the same problems of educating their children as missionaries coming from overseas, and with far slenderer financial resources. The National Missionary Society only exists because of the strong missionary enthusiasm which exists in so many of the churches of India, and hundreds of examples of local evangelism especially by women could be quoted. The following comes from the Women's Home Missionary Society in the hill country of Assam: 'Our women take up a collection which is a handful of rice set apart from each meal. This handful of rice at the end of the week comes to about two pounds. This is brought to church and later sold at a little cheaper rate for the support of our evangelists. Evangelistic campaigns are organised and the women go out in groups of forty or fifty for a period of corporate witness.' The Kyodan Fujinbu, the Women's organisation of the Church of Japan, also organises evangelistic campaigns and meetings. In fact, one may say that in most places where social customs make a joint evangelistic approach to men and women difficult, women carry on evangelistic work.

One of the most remarkable of women's movements is that which has grown among the Batak people in Sumatra in the last twenty years. The whole story of the building of the Batak Church out of an independent, warlike and savage people is one of the miracles of missionary work. The work among women began when a Dutch woman missionary, rather against the advice of her colleagues, began as a spare time occupation, over and above her work in a town school for girls, to visit the surrounding villages. She used her holidays to go to each village for a week at a time and conduct simple Bible teaching. Women flocked to hear her and soon there were regular groups in many villages. The problem was how to shepherd these groups. After great difficulties a building was obtained for starting a Bible school in which to train women as leaders. The conditions were so inauspicious, the people so new to the faith that visitors came from far and wide to see the school as something of a marvel. The course included Bible study, housekeeping, gardening and Sunday School training. It opened in 1934 and seventy women had been trained when the war broke out and the school had to be closed. The majority of the women were married, and the understanding was that each woman would do what she could in her own place. When the war was over a remarkable work had been done by these women, and strong women's groups were built up which were ready to send missionaries to remoter parts, and all were financially self-supporting. The particular interest of this report is the training of women for voluntary leadership. It was indeed a case of 'casting bread upon the waters' for there was no guarantee that these trained women would do what was hoped, they had no pay, no supervision and no terms of employment. Perhaps the Churches elsewhere are too ready to assume that the natural outcome of training is full-time employment.

Hand in hand with an enthusiasm for evangelism goes genuinely sacrificial giving. This is to be found in the West too, but nowhere does it equal the really hard pinching that goes into such offerings as these: 'The women regularly tithe their resources, taking over into the Church the age-old Indian custom of giving a tenth of the crops. Even a cook earning $10 a month gives her tithe to women's work' (Nicaragua). 'Every egg laid by their hens on Sundays is brought to the Church' (Philippines). 'An offering of the talents is made: a hen perhaps is given and the eggs laid by it throughout the year are given to the work, or the women make and sell goods' (Cuba).

E

The events of the last ten years in the war and the tremendous need for post-war reconstruction have made women everywhere aware of the sufferings of others and anxious to help them. To countless women the ecumenical movement has become a reality through the work of the Department of Reconstruction and Inter-Church Aid of the World Council of Churches. A small group of women in Basrah, for example, say they get real encouragement in their work of making clothes and collecting goods in the realisation that countless American women are doing the same. South American women write of their efforts to befriend refugees from Europe, and remote groups of women in different parts of the world have made their offerings through their parent Churches. Some have felt that the outside world was a reality for the first time when men from their villages went overseas in the war. This is especially mentioned in the report from India.

It is striking to notice how very many women's movements keep the Women's World Day of Prayer on the first Friday in Lent. For many women this is the only means open to them of expressing their relationship to other Christian women and their sole knowledge of what other women in different parts of the world do and think. The movement for keeping this day is steadily gaining in strength.

Some women's organisations have powerful links with Churches of their own communions overseas. This is especially true of the Mothers' Union, which supports missionary work of its own and has women of all races in its membership. It is also true of the Methodists, who have the most thoroughly organised of all women's movements, partly perhaps because they are a young Church with a connexional organisation running through every aspect of their work. The Lutheran Churches of America also have a keen sense of confessional loyalty, expressed, for example, in the highly organised and generously supported work of the Lutheran World Federation for impoverished Lutheran Churches in Europe, and displaced persons and refugees both in Europe and elsewhere. For all Churches these confessional ties across national boundaries have been strengthened by the war. For women's movements they give the same outlet for service as the foreign mission enterprise. One report contains the comment that it is easier to feel ecumenical towards members of your own confession thousands of miles away than towards a group in the same town of a different denomination.

Are women's movements more readily disposed to think and act ecumenically than the Churches they belong to? In one sense less: some movements are more conservative than the leadership of their Churches, their literature tends to be filled with their own concerns. Women, it is said, are interested in works, but not in the Faith and Order aspect of the ecumenical movement. Theologically educated women, mostly outside the women's movements, have an almost inevitable interest in the ecumenical movement. There are only a few of them, their place in their own Churches is often ill-defined and insecure and they want to know what is happening in other Churches, to meet other women, and questions of Faith and Order have a strong personal interest for them. In women's church movements women want to know about other women, but it is not a matter of urgency with them. Women's movements have a strong influence on their Churches in social matters and on questions of Christian morality, but in matters of Faith and Order they have no influence because they have no experience. On the other hand, just because women have less part in committing their Churches ecumenically, they are sometimes willing to come together in an ecumenical women's movement when the Church to which they belong will not. So it comes about that the strongest developments towards joint activity between women's movements are concerned with social service and with the relation of church women to the community. Far more has been done along these lines in the United States than anywhere else. Some of these inter-denominational councils are the women's departments of local Councils of Churches. Some have grown out of work for Home and Foreign Missions and are the women's groups connected with the Foreign Mission Conference and the Home Missions Council. The United Council of Church Women was organised in 1941 to bring together these inter-denominational groups, but in 1950 merged with the parent bodies of these other women's organisations into the new National Christian Council of the United States. The relations between the women's group and the local Council of Churches are not always easy, especially if, as frequently happens, the Council of Churches consists entirely of men, of whom nearly all are clergy.

The United Council of Church Women has done a notable service in standing firmly against race discrimination. Its board includes Negro, Chinese, Japanese and American Indian women, and it has done an educative work among its constituent bodies, especially in working for peace, stimulating action in local communities and sponsoring the observance of the Women's World Day of Prayer.

Many local councils of women have worked for all kinds of social ends, and especially for better race relations. It takes courage in the deep South for white women to sit through the trials of negroes because they know that their presence will make for a cleaner trial, or to protest against the lack of housing and education for negroes. This they did. But just in so far as women's ecumenical groups draw together women from a wider range than the Churches and concentrate largely on social ends, they raise the question, what is their relation to the Churches? And many of the projects on which they work successfully would not exclude the co-operation of Jews and Mohammedans—indeed, there are countries in the world where co-operation is either on an interfaith basis or not at all, and often it is the secular organisation which provides the framework within which Christian women can come to know each other. This is mentioned in reports from Egypt, Syria and India, where often it is the Red Cross or Red Crescent Society which is the means of joint working.

It must be borne in mind that this question of joint working only arises in any serious form where there are a number of Churches of more or less equal strength, as in the United States and the British Empire. In most countries of Europe one Protestant Church is in a position of great strength and there are small minorities with which it may or may not enter into relationship. For such Churches ecumenical must of necessity mean international also. In Great Britain co-operation between women's movements takes the form of a consultative committee of women's church organisations, newly established. In New Zealand there is a woman's committee of the National Council of Churches. The part played by the Women's World Day of Prayer in stimulating ecumenical activity in South Africa has already been quoted.

Under this heading mention can be made of a particular question affecting those countries which contain in their populations more than one race. On the whole the attitude of women's organisations is more liberal than that of society at large, and more liberal often than the general attitude prevailing in the Churches. Many women's movements have branches for races other than those of the main membership. It is sometimes suspected that this separation is a form of race discrimination. One reason for separate branches is difference of language, and this operates between groups of the same race: thus for example, the main reason why there is not more co-operation between Dutch Reformed and other denominational women's groups in South Africa is that few women of the former group speak anything but Afrikaans. Most of the women's movements give equal voting powers to non-European branches. However, a difficulty arises in that African women, as they gain in education and in experience of serving on committees, want to run their own organisation where they need not be under the leadership of Europeans. The Methodist women's organisation in South Africa has come to the conclusion, after most careful thought, that this is the right course for their African members.

A DIFFERENT PATTERN OF WOMEN'S CHURCH WORK

All the work of women's voluntary organisations which has so far been discussed has had one feature in common, in spite of many differences. Whether it has been highly organised or rather loosely organised, all the work has been directly linked with the Church and, with the exception of the interdenominational work just described, each organisation has belonged to one particular Church and much of the work done by the women has used church premises, at any rate locally.

But there are some countries in which this 'overall' type of women's organisation is practically if not completely unknown. Correspondents in these countries were obviously hard put to it to know how to answer the questions in this section of their reports. The difference may be summarised thus. In Norway, Denmark and Sweden there are national Churches closely linked to the State, and this makes for a different relationship between the Church and society from that prevailing in almost any other

country. The second factor in the difference is that in these
countries and also in Holland, Germany, and, to a certain extent,
Switzerland the Home Mission has developed very strongly.
Different autonomous bodies organise and carry out different
types of social work with a strong religious bias, staffed by persons trained in Christian training institutions, especially in the
deaconess training houses. Groups of women support this work
as voluntary helpers and as subscribers, and the various societies
which come under the name 'Home Mission' may be as diverse as
the Bible Society and a hospital for epileptics.

To take the first point—the different relation between Church
and society in countries where there is a national Church closely
linked to the State:

The Norwegian report explains the matter clearly in the following way: 'Because the Norwegian State Church has no basis of
personal membership as those Churches have in which grown-up
people enlist by their own action, it is rather hard to define the
expression "Church Women". Congregations are geographically
confined. Every new-born child of a family belonging to the
State Church is, with the act of baptism, put on the church roll.
Every Norwegian citizen who has not formally expressed the
intention of leaving the Church is a member for life. Accordingly
every organised body of women members of the Lutheran State
Church who are doing work in any field of Christian activity must
be looked on as a group of church women, even if they have not
been organised through the action of the church leaders and are
not in direct touch with the Church as such.' The report goes on
to describe what actually happens. There are local groups of
women within the congregations who work for the sick and the
poor, and help to support local efforts for orphans and the aged.
But most women's groups are attached to some central voluntary
Christian movement, such as the Norwegian Missionary Society,
the Mission to Seamen, the Home Mission, the Sunday School
Association or national organisations such as exist for women
teachers to interest them in missions, for telephonists and for
nurses. Most of these organisations, except the last three mentioned, are not women's organisations, and on their boards women
are represented very sparsely, if at all, above the level of the local
group. On the other hand, and perhaps for the very reason that
this is the situation in regard to women's work, the Y.W.C.A. is

much more closely linked with the Church in Norway than it is in many other countries, and seems to take the place, for many women, of the women's voluntary organisation as it has been described above.

The Danish report, which omits the section on the Voluntary Organisations of women in the Church, describes much the same situation as the Norwegian. Groups of women work for the Home Mission and for Foreign Missions, and one woman serves on the Northern Missionary Committee (Norway, Sweden and Denmark). The Home Mission in Denmark is connected with the Fellowship Movement, an evangelical movement for the recovery of personal faith. Men and women, paid and voluntary, work together organising clubs and sending women workers into the factories in Copenhagen. The Church Army of the Cross sends men and women all over the country on evangelistic and social missions and they speak in churches, hold night missions, visit public houses and run convalescent homes, camps and kindergartens. There is not the same difference in Denmark between what in other countries would be called church movements of women and secular movements. It is characteristic of the country that many of its voluntary movements have been founded by men and women of deep Christian faith and retain their Christian character to a marked degree; this is true, for example, of the famous Folk High Schools. For this reason our correspondent in Denmark describes groups of housekeepers in villages, somewhat like the British Women's Institutes. But whereas in the British movement the discussion of any religious subject is banned by the constitution of the movement, in Denmark there are village groups in which domestic subjects and Bible study both have their place.

In Sweden the same relationship, or very nearly, between Church and State and Church and society pertains as in Norway and Denmark. Here also there are no large-scale women's organisations in the Church, nor in the Swedish Mission Covenant, which is a gathered community of a Congregationalist nature with some 1,640 congregations and its own ministry, but whose members have not contracted out of the State Church. The sewing guilds are universal. For the most part they are started by the minister, and his wife usually has a large share in the organisation. The minister leads, as a rule, an opening devotional session, and a book is read while the women sew, and there is coffee and discussion when the work is put away. The Scandinavian countries are the only ones in which the original 'Ladies Aid' or 'Dorcas Society' of so many congregations in so many communions persist as the main type of women's work. That the work of the sewing guilds is harnessed to modern needs is shown by the number of causes which are supported—local needs, home mission work among the Lapps, foreign missionary work, institutions of all kinds, and a very large volume of support has flowed from these groups to relieve the sufferings of the people of Europe, both during and since the war, while war orphans in considerable numbers have been accepted and cared for. The burden has been very heavy, 'but', says the report, 'there is no parish so small and poor as not to be wonderfully inexhaustible both as to strength and as to funds'. Two questions have been left unsolved by this type of women's work, one, the provision of teaching and training in the faith and in Christian leadership for the more or less educated woman, the other the question of the relation of Christian women to the many and strong secular movements among women which thrive in Sweden. The first question had not been wholly neglected, for at least two societies worked to interest educated women, including students, in missionary work, one the Swedish Women's Missionary Society and the other the Missionary Society of Teachers, which in Sweden has had a very successful history, keeping no less than sixteen women missionaries and twenty-three Bible women in China, Mongolia, India and Africa.

A development more closely bound to the Church, is that of Women's Diocesan Councils, appointed by the Diocesan Councils of the Church of Sweden in which clergy and laity (including women) sit together. The aim of these diocesan councils of women is to be working teams to inspire and instruct church women, and to evangelise among those outside the Church. They organise meetings and courses of various kinds, lectures, contact conferences, instruction days, etc. The first of these councils was founded by the wife of the then Bishop of Härnösand, Mrs. Anna Bohlin, and other dioceses have followed. Arising out of the success of this work in so many dioceses a conference was held in 1947, and the second question was discussed—how could the women of the Church make their voice heard in some of the large women's conferences in Sweden in which the Church had no voice because there was no organisation to be represented. As a result the Church of Sweden Central Council of Women was founded 'as a central organ for women's work within the Church and as a representation outwards'. (The Central Council for Women's Work in the Church of England, with its diocesan organisation, has the same function.)

In Holland much women's service is canalised through the Y.W.C.A. or through branches of the Home Mission. The reason for this lies partly in the structure of the Dutch Church, (meaning by this the Dutch Reformed Church, which is the national Church but ceased to be the State Church in 1795), and also of those Churches or groups which at various times have broken away from it on questions of the authority of the Bible rather than on questions of church order. Partly also the reason is to be found in the relation of the Church to society in a country so nearly equally divided between Roman Catholic and Protestant as Holland is. The Dutch Reformed Church has preserved the ancient doctrine that one of the functions of the Church is *diaconia* in the sense of practical service to the members of the Christian community, and it has preserved also an order of ministry, the diaconate, whose task it is to administer the funds given by the congregations for the poor. Some early communities of the Reformed tradition did in fact have women deacons. But in the Reformed Church itself there are no women deacons. The deacons (who serve for a township and not for an individual congregation in a town) do employ women social workers, but the fact that what could have been the social work of the Church carried on by men and women has become entirely a man's preserve has probably had something to do with immensely strong development of Home Mission work under autonomous boards not under the control of any church councils. In these boards a certain number of women serve, and an immense number of women are enrolled in local branches to support the work. A social factor has also entered in to reinforce the strength of the Home Mission. In a country in which there are to be found Protestant and Catholic political parties (and more than one of each), Protestant and Catholic Trades Unions, Protestant and Catholic radio stations, it is not surprising to find Protestant homes for the aged (it is estimated that there are 300 in Holland under the Home Mission alone), Protestant hospitals, tuberculosis clinics and mental homes.

The work included under the title 'Home Missions' includes also moral welfare work among prostitutes and morally endangered girls, railway mission work, two court missions for work among prisoners, a hundred and fifty or so foster societies for adopting children, two large tuberculosis clinics, a home for epileptics, nine societies for the care of mentally defective children and adults, some twelve hospitals for the insane, including seven thousand women patients, and, beside all this, work for cripples, the blind, the deaf and for sickly children. Much of the work receives government financial aid, but even so there is an army of voluntary subscribers from all the Protestant Churches. Professional women, many of them trained either in the deaconess training centres or in the Christian schools of training for social work, staff many of these institutions. 'There are thousands of them,' the report concludes, 'varying from home evangelists to assistants in orphanages. There are tens of thousands of women who take in one way or another an active part in some branch of home mission work, and hundreds of thousands who give financial support to it.'

The effect of the German occupation was to make some of these organisations come rather closer to the Church, almost the only free society which the occupying powers did not try to close down, and some at least of the Home Mission societies are now wondering what their future relationship to the Church ought to be. The Church has also been thinking since the war about its own special responsibilities in the field of social work, and a special council has been set up to deal with family problems, called the Council for Church and Family. The war opened opportunities for a drawing together of the Church and society in Holland such as came to very few Churches, and use was made of it to create new instruments for the Church to serve the community better. There are also meetings for women, mostly for mothers, within the congregations. 'Since the war,' writes a Dutch correspondent, 'two groups of women's organisations, one of those from the liberal congregations and one of those from the orthodox, are in the midst of an interesting growth; not only in numbers but also in the consciousness of being the women's groups within the Church and having a responsibility as such. It is only a beginning, especially in the orthodox groups, but it is real. Their programme is still very simple, but it is expanding. Another hopeful side of the development, new in the last year, is the growing understanding and co-operation between these two groups. This is, I think, the first instance of organisations of church members, organised definitely along these (i.e. liberal and orthodox) lines seeking deliberately to come closer to each other.'

In Germany also a great deal of women's church work is voluntary work attached to one or another branch of Home Mission work. The Reichsfrauenhilfe, with some one to one and a half million members, has women's groups within the congregation, whose chief purpose is Bible study and so is part of the Church, but which, as a registered charitable society for social work, is also part of the Home Mission. Another women's movement, the Evangelische Frauenbund, is aimed at the more educated churchwomen. In most of the Länder (provinces) there are committees of the provincial Church which draw together women's work; some are thoroughly organised with a committee under the bishop (like Hanover and Baden), while others (Nassau-Hessen) are purely consultative. At the centre the Evangelische Frauenarbeit (evangelical women's work) draws together work done by women both voluntarily and professionally, through the Churches and through the Home Mission, including the provincial organisations, and arranges conferences for women to meet and discuss their work. All this work came very heavily under the heel of the Nazis, whose aim was to make every form of social work a part of the State under their control.

The days in which the Church was the only, or almost the only, institution to educate and help the poor, the sick, the needy and the aged have passed away. The provision of education and medical care on a scale adequate for whole populations is costly beyond the means of private bodies. Everywhere the responsibility for meeting these needs is passing to the whole community, which operates through the agency of the State and local government. Home Missions, especially as they have survived in Holland, still carry a large share in making these social provisions, but for the most part they are heavily subsidised by the State, and everywhere there are small institutions where the Churches still have a direct responsibility for some piece of social or educational work. In some places they exercise their influence through the training of teachers and nurses, but in spite of that the broad picture is the same: social provisions are made by society not by the Churches.

What is the Church's unique and specific contribution now? This is a question which particularly concerns women, because they form the greatest part of the army of social workers and teachers which society employs. It most particularly affects those women who want to make their life work the service of God, and have to ask: shall it be church work or shall it be social work in non-church institutions? To their questions we must turn next.

III

FULL-TIME AND PROFESSIONAL SERVICE
OF WOMEN IN THE CHURCH

THIS TITLE is a necessarily misleading one. No phrase will cover the range of service to be included in this section, for both 'full-time' and 'professional' include a great variety of types of service. At the one extreme is the nun whose vows commit her to a life-time's devotion (without salary) and at the other is the nurse or teacher trained in the deaconess establishment who may be working in an institution not under the Church and paid by the State or the locality, and the religious education instructor in Church or school who is trained and probably paid by the Church but may not do this work for more than a few years. Where also can a place be found in neat pigeon-holes for the chief burden-bearer in local work among church women, the unpaid but often highly trained mainstay of the parish, who has every kind of duty and no kind of status—the parson's wife?

Several of the reports on the full-time or professional work of women for the Churches, including those from the United States and Germany, say that it is quite impossible either to give full details of the kind of work being done or to count heads. 'No one knows,' says the American report, 'how many women today are employed by the American Churches in different types of activities. There are professional workers, women ministers, missionaries (home and foreign), deaconesses, executives and field workers in denominational and inter-denominational organisations, directors of religious education, physicians, nurses and technicians in church hospitals, social workers, teachers and writers and editors of church periodicals. That is only a partial list.'

The only thing to do, therefore, in this section is to describe what the main recognizable types of women workers are doing,

with the warning that much may have been omitted.[1] A confusion
of terms as between different countries and Churches, most particularly of the use of the word 'ordained' and the different kinds
of service and status implied by the word 'deaconess', makes for
further difficulties of classification and those who wish to compare
what women do in one Church with what they do in another must
think in terms of the status and function of different types of
workers and not rely on the names given to them. A further
confusion is caused by the fact that very few Churches have made
up their collective minds on what they think about the place of
women in the Church. Nearly all of them contain conservatives
and liberals in this matter, in differing proportions. Few are prepared to add one more to the number of debatable matters which
threaten their unity of opinion. Yet most Churches are under some
sort of pressure of circumstance, compelling principle to make
compromise with events. In all there are to be found small
bodies of men and women working to obtain a place for women
to use their gifts in the service of the Church, who obtain from
time to time at least partial success in their efforts. The result of
this lack of a clear mind is to destroy exact definition of the status
and function of women workers, and to make clear classification
and comparison between Churches quite impossible. For nearly
all Churches in effect say 'women may serve in these and these
ways, and will be called deaconesses or lay workers or directors of
religious education, and in exceptional circumstances they may do
this or this with authority from such and such'. But the functions
are differently defined and limited from Church to Church:
emergencies differently conceived, and the authority under whom
the woman works may be the local minister, a board or a bishop.
In fact, anyone who approaches a study of Faith and Order with
the laity of the Churches mainly in mind is driven to the conclusion that a division of a Church into two parts, 'ministry' and
'laity' clearly and absolutely divided in status and function is
impossible. Orthodox Churches make a clear distinction between
'priesthood' and 'laity', but with a large variety of 'ministries'
within the laity. A small but significant number of church members do not fall completely into either category. A large proportion

[1] No attempt will be made to deal with the very large number of women
who work in church offices and Christian organisations as typists, ac-
countants, etc.

of this class[1] are women whose status and functions have been defined to give them a quasi-ministerial position in the Churches.

The method of classification which follows (in so far as it can be described either as a method or as a classification) takes the historical development of different types of work as the key to their present place in the Church. Although under pressure a Church may accept unusual service from women, an effort is always made at the time or afterwards either to abolish the form of service accepted in emergency or to justify and regularise it by an appeal to Scripture and to church tradition. The nearer a service of women approaches to the ministerial function, the more on edge the Churches are about it. The question of women in the ministry at once raises every other question on which there are divided counsels in most Churches—the authority of the Bible and the criteria for its interpretation for modern needs, the nature of the ministry, the relation of ministry and laity, the autonomy of the local congregation, and added to all this the age-old question of the relation of religion and sex which still exercises a powerful influence largely inexpressible in words. For this reason, and because the Churches have given more earnest study to this question than to any other, the matter will be dealt with in a separate chapter. The Scottish report remarks that 'it would be unfortunate if in present-day discussions of women's service too great prominence should be given to the claim that women should be eligible for ordination to the Holy Ministry on the same terms as men. The effect of this might be to retard the development of other lines of Christian activity in which women might play a great and distinctive part'. Few Churches have seriously discussed the effect on church policy and even on church order of such work of women as has already developed.

THE DEACONESSES

The first chapter of this book showed how in the Eastern Church the deaconess performed an important function and held an honoured status. Her task was to care especially for the women and children of the Church, to give help to the poor and needy

---

[1] Churches of the Reformed tradition which regard the eldership as a form of ministry have a large class of men who, though laity, are ordained to their office.

and to teach, especially in the homes of the people. Her high status was symbolised by her ordination at the hands of a bishop and her service at the altar in administering the chalice at Holy Communion. In the West opinions about the service of deaconesses were divided in the pre-Reformation Church and women found a greater place in the Church through the abbeys and nunneries than they did in the parishes.

The revival of the idea of deaconesses in the post-Reformation Churches has resulted in three types of deaconess, of which the first two here described are clearly distinguishable from each other, and the third is nearer the second than the first. The first in order of appearance is the German deaconess belonging to one or other of the great deaconess mother houses stemming from the revival of deaconess work in the early nineteenth century. Her training is primarily that of a nurse (or less usually teacher) with Bible study and certain other subjects also, and she works as a nurse (or, much more rarely, as a teacher). These orders of deaconesses are in their relation to the Church not within and part of church order but alongside it. The second type of deaconess is the Anglican. Her training is theological, her work is mainly a teaching ministry, usually exercised in the parish. She is ordained by laying on of hands by a bishop and the Anglican order of deaconesses is a recognised order of ministry within the framework of church order. The third type of deaconess, of the Baptist, Methodist and Presbyterian Churches, corresponds closely to the 'parish assistant' of the Reformed and Lutheran Churches, and to the 'parish worker' of the Anglican Church, working within a parish especially in the teaching of women and children and under the direction of the minister or of the parish board. More modern developments within the framework of the first deaconess movement have led to the training of this type of worker. Churches which have never had the first type of deaconess do have orders of deaconesses of this third type, and in other Churches what is called a parish worker or a pastor's assistant approximates in function to this type of deaconess. In some Churches this third type of deaconess receives nursing training but for the most part they are not nurses or trained teachers.

The revival of deaconesses in Germany in the first part of the last century is, in terms of its subsequent influence, the greatest event in the life of women in the Church since the Reformation. It took place in a little village on the Rhine called Kaiserswerth, a predominantly Catholic village to which a young pastor was sent in 1822 to shepherd a tiny congregation of Protestants, the work-people in a recently transported velvet industry. A disastrous failure in the industry sent young Pastor Fliedner abroad, raising funds for help, and on his journeys he visited England. Being already keenly interested in the condition of the people and the inadequacy of public institutions, he visited prisons and reformatories and went to see Newgate, where Elizabeth Fry was doing her revolutionary work among women prisoners. He did not see her, but returned home full of her achievements and at once visited the prison in Düsseldorf near Kaiserswerth. He was appalled both at the physical conditions and at the lack of any kind of attempt to enable prisoners to make good when discharged. He collected statistics from different parts of Germany to show the very high proportion of illiterates among prisoners, got the government to consent to the appointment of chaplains and schoolmasters in prisons, and formed a society on the lines of what he had seen in England. One of his chief supporters in the struggle for this reform (and he had many enemies) was the local Roman Catholic priest, and it is perhaps not fanciful to suppose that through Roman Catholic friends he at least heard of the Sisters of Mercy, founded many years ago by St. Vincent de Paul and now a powerful movement. He then turned to the question of help for the sick poor, pitifully ill-provided for. He went abroad again in 1832, this time paid for by the Ministry of Education. On this visit to England he did meet Elizabeth Fry, but if he hoped for any ideas on hospitals from England he got nothing but warnings, and commented on the contrast between the handsome buildings, and the wretched condition of the patients left to the tender mercies of women whose nursing skill was negligible and who were, many of them, nothing more than drunkards and prostitutes. Back he came to take over the house of the merchant, whose business had failed. The outcry against the coming of 'a plague spot' to the middle of the town was terrific, but in the first year Fliedner had forty patients and seven women to nurse them, and he had a physician in charge. These women he called deaconesses. While the physician taught them how to care for the sick, Fliedner taught them to study their Bibles, helped them as a chaplain with their own spiritual life, and was there to assist them as they tried to meet the spiritual needs of the patients.

The astonishing thing about this new movement was the speed with which it grew. The age of building institutions for the sick, poor and orphaned had begun, but there were few trained helpers. So from Holland, Switzerland and France women were sent for training, and demands came for the supply of deaconesses. In 1849 Fliedner took four deaconesses to America; three years later another party accompanied him to Jerusalem, and soon hospitals and schools in Constantinople, Smyrna, Alexandria, Bucharest and Florence were staffed by nurses and teachers trained in Kaiserswerth. All this time the institution itself was growing in size, and an orphanage, a school, a home for discharged women prisoners and an asylum were added to the original building. It was the desire to care for neglected children which led Fliedner to the establishment of a school where teachers were trained. The nurses went out either to nurse in hospitals or in private families, or to work in parishes as visiting nurses among the parishioners.

New training institutions on the Kaiserswerth model sprang up all over Germany. But Fliedner's work was not the only, though it was certainly the greatest, inspiration in this movement. The ecumenical character of it all, the way in which ideas and impulses spread from one country and Church to another is remarkable. The idea of reviving the office of deaconess in the Church was present in the minds of a number of people at about the same time. A certain Pastor Clönne of Bislich near Wesel proposed the idea as early as 1817. He was anxious to revive it as a spiritual office and on a scriptural basis. A number of eminent men supported the idea and it was thought that it would be a fitting way of celebrating the tercentenary of the Reformation, which fell in that year. Wesel had been connected with the last revival of the office of deaconess, for certain Dutch congregations fled to Cleves in the sixteenth century to escape persecution, and founded there what were called the 'secret communities beneath the cross'. In all their sufferings the members of these communities supported each other and the women acting as deaconesses were the agents of this mutual help. The Convention of Wesel in 1568 regularised an office of deaconesses, and older women were consecrated to this office and to the care of the poor and sick. The office lapsed, probably when the communities began to accept aid for the sick and poor from the civic authorities. Although Clönne did not succeed in his immediate object, his thought was known widely, and certainly to Fliedner.

Another seemingly independent source of inspiration came from England, where, in the early years of the century, an English clergyman wrote to the Bishop of London, suggesting that a Protestant counterpart of the Roman Catholic Sisters of Mercy should be founded in London. His plans were carefully worked out. He wanted to have women living together in a house where they would be trained by clergy in Bible study and pastoral care of the sick, and from which they would go out to hospitals to be trained in nursing by the doctors. The new order was to be run by a Board which would look after the sisters in sickness and old age. This plan, which foreshadowed in a remarkable way nearly all the features of the deaconess mother houses as they subsequently developed, got no further than the early nineteenth century equivalent of a bishop's 'pending' tray. Probably the idea of the sisters smacked too much of Rome for the Bishop's liking, but even had he been prepared to look at the proposal favourably he would have found a check in the terrible condition of the hospitals. This was the one difference between this plan and what subsequently developed in Germany, that the deaconess institute at Kaiserswerth and most other training institutes had their own hospitals. However, copies of the English plan travelled abroad, and in 1827 Nicolas Heinrich Julius published a pamphlet in Berlin which was very widely read. In it he explained and commended the English scheme, described the work of Elizabeth Fry, and added to it an account of work of the 'Compassionate Widows', founded in St. Petersburg in 1814 by Maria Fedorovna, widow of the Czar. Unquestionably the times were favourable for a revival of the work of women in the Church. Fanatical prejudice against anything which corresponded in any particular to a Romish practice had abated, and the terrible conditions of poverty and distress following the Napoleonic wars called for an outpouring of Christian charity and service. But the Christian can hardly fail to see in the stirring of a similar impulse within communions so different as the Roman Catholic, Russian Orthodox, Anglican, Reformed and Lutheran the marks of a movement of the Spirit.

The principles of the deaconess movement, as it developed in Germany, can be very simply described. All the work is centred on the mother houses. Here the young sisters are trained and are on probation. Most of the mother houses have their own hospital, in which the nursing training is given. Some give nothing more than a general nursing training, others give specialised courses in different branches of nursing and in hospital management, dietetics or physio-therapy. All deaconesses receive regular instruction in Bible study and in the spiritual care of patients. Some mother houses also train deaconesses as children's nurses and as teachers. The deaconesses wear a uniform, they are given pocket money, and if they are employed in institutions which pay salaries, their salary goes to their mother house. The mother house cares for its deaconesses in sickness and old age and also provides holidays for the sisters. Deaconesses resign on marriage. The mother house exercises discipline over the deaconess both in training and afterwards, in accordance with a rule. The degree of closeness to the Church varies very much from Church to Church and country to country. As a general rule when deaconesses are consecrated it is as members of their order and not as servants of the Church.

Germany has remained the stronghold of the deaconess movement. Here there are two main orders of deaconesses. Much the larger is the Kaiserswerther, composed of four unions of deaconess mother houses, scattered throughout Germany. These unions draw into a loose fellowship mother houses which have fairly close affinities in rule and in training. The number of sisters belonging to this order is given as 30,000. The period of training and testing is six to seven years. The other main order is the Zehlendorfer with its headquarters in Berlin. A much larger proportion of these sisters have a secondary school training and about 14 per cent. of them have matriculated. They have three years training in sick nursing and two in infant care and sit for the State examinations. They are dedicated as deaconesses after six to eight years of proof of character and technical competence. The sisters of this order are also trained to be wives and mothers, and they retire on marriage. They receive a salary and provide their own clothes, and they wear uniform. They work in hospitals, institutions and as parish nurses. Their numbers are given as about 3,300.

In other countries to which the deaconess movement has spread the work is much the same and the conditions of membership of the orders vary very little. There are twenty deaconess houses in

Holland, (sixteen belonging to a union of deaconess houses), four in Sweden (that in Stockholm was founded in 1851), four in Switzerland under the National Church (the earliest founded in 1842) with 2,400 sisters, and eight under the Free Churches with 1,430 sisters, and in addition there is a Red Cross and a sick nursing institute. In Norway there are two deaconess mother houses with 800 sisters; in Denmark three with 800 sisters. There are five mother houses in France, the three largest have about a hundred sisters each and the others are very small; one in Austria with 250 sisters, four in Hungary, and four in Finland with between thirteen and fourteen hundred sisters. The figures for the number of sisters where given include sisters no longer working, and sisters in training, but do not include those who have left their orders for marriage or for any other reason. There are no vows binding deaconesses to a lifetime of service.

Deaconess houses were established in America at the end of the nineteenth century as the result of the influence of the German example, and in those Churches which were nearest to the continental pattern of churchmanship. The number of deaconesses is small by comparison with Europe, ten Lutheran bodies in America having a total of 386 in active service. The Evangelical and Reformed Church has a small number working in deaconess hospitals and on the mission field. It may be fairly taken for granted that the missionary societies of the countries so far named have at least a few deaconesses working with them in the foreign field, but the numbers are in no case stated, though mention is made of them in the reports.

Nearly all the reports mention certain difficulties, and some of these difficulties are common to all countries. The position of women in society has changed very greatly since Fliedner began his work. Almost everywhere there is questioning about whether deaconesses ought to be compelled to wear uniform, and relaxations of the rule are common, the deaconesses being allowed to wear ordinary clothes when off duty. This feeling against uniform takes a stronger form in the French report, where the writer, herself a member of a deaconess order, says that in a country which is half Catholic and half anti-clerical the wearing of uniform by Protestant sisters is bound to be misunderstood by the people among whom they work. On the whole the questioning about the wearing of uniform is not a thing in itself, but a symptom of something else, of the desire to be more closely identified with those who serve society in much the same ways but without being separate from it. Frequently the question is asked why a nurse who is a deaconess should not receive the same pay as a nurse who is not. For this reason a new scheme has been drawn up in Norway for the payment of deaconesses on a salary basis. It is not easy to work out equality, says the Swedish report, because the work differs so much. In Switzerland, and perhaps elsewhere, deaconesses keep their own private property. For every young woman who considers whether she ought to become a deaconess there is the strong attraction of other forms of social service which seem to offer the same opportunities of serving but with fewer restrictions on personal liberty. Some young women feel that the discipline of the mother house is too rigid, and question whether a trained deaconess should be sent to a job chosen by the mother house. 'It seems,' says the Norwegian report, 'as if the rather stiff system of the mother house will have to be moderated, but the important part it has always played in creating the spirit of unity, service and sisterhood must not be lost.' Yet another difficulty is the attitude of the Church towards the work of the deaconess. She is expected to be the uncomplaining slave. A strong expression of this view is quoted in the American report coming from the head of a Lutheran mother house in America, who spoke of 'the degree of subservience expected of a deaconess, carried to extreme in opposition to the advanced education of deaconesses for fear they will no longer be willing to do so-called menial tasks'.

Nearly everywhere it is reported that there are more demands for deaconesses to work in the hospitals of their orders, in those of other organisations or of the State, in special institutions for the handicapped, and in parochial nursing, than there are recruits to fill the places. One reason for the increase in demand is, says the Swiss report, the restriction of hours that nurses may work, with the consequence that a far larger number are needed. Most countries report a difficulty, if not in getting a sufficient number of recruits, in getting recruits with sufficient educational and cultural background. 'Most of the deaconesses come from the country, very few from cultured homes. The demand is great for persons with better education for leading positions,' (Finland). 'Most of our deaconesses come from the less well-educated classes of the community. The more cultured girls do not feel at home as deaconesses,' (Austria). 'Most of the deaconesses now come from simple circumstances, from the country and so on,' (Sweden). 'Many come from domestic service, shops, hotels, industry and agriculture, and from mental, children's and public hospitals. Occasionally teachers offer their service,' (Switzerland). It seems fairly clear from the reports that where a mother house offers a higher standard of training it gets more of the type of women needed. No mention is made of a factor to which all young women have to give attention nowadays. They cannot think of their vocation as individuals, they have to think of their families, and whereas there used to be in Europe a large middle class with sufficient means to support parents in old age and emergency, and leave daughters free to work for nothing but their keep, many young women now have to take into account the fact that they may have to help support their families, and that unless they are as highly trained in youth as their capacity allows, they will be unlikely in middle-age to find jobs with salaries adequate to keep more than one person. Some of the reports show signs of having been written by older persons who think that the motives of the young in seeking higher pay are entirely selfish. Probably the Dutch report more accurately reflects the opinions of the young when it says: 'There are several reasons why more developed girls from Christian homes do not join the deaconesses. The work is too one-sided (mostly nursing). The financial aspect is unsatisfactory. The work is so heavy that only the very strong can maintain it. There is too little free time for repose and development, for lectures, concerts and sport. Deaconesses are put much under restraint. Being a deaconess requires restraint, but there are still many remains of the pietistical style of life with its many commandments and prohibitions—"a good deaconess does not do this or that", or "formerly deaconesses lived so much for their patients that they scarcely knew what was going on in the world". This is no recommendation for girls and women today who are conscious of their responsibility in the world. They do not want human commandments put up as though they were divine. The restraint of the Home is often felt as a handicap to the work, preventing one from giving oneself wholly to it.'

Changes in training are slowly beginning to take place, not only because higher technical skills are needed. The whole idea behind deaconess training is that the sister should have time as she nurses to attend to the spiritual needs of her patients, for which she has been specially trained. The Swiss report comments that the pace of nursing in a modern institution is so fast that there is not time for this sort of work. This means that the woman to whom the attraction of deaconess work is the opportunity for spiritual work which it gives often wants to go into other work where there will be time for it. There is more time for it in parochial work (district nursing and church social work). Here too she is more closely identified as the servant of the Church. The result of this is that there are within several deaconess orders, houses which are specialising in training for parish work, with a larger share of time given to theological studies. Norway has a mother house for the training of parish sisters, founded in 1936 and steadily growing in numbers. In Sweden some deaconesses are sent from other houses to the mother house in Upsala so that they can read theology at the university. The report on deaconesses from this country ends with the remark that the increasing secularisation of the State's social service is leading more deaconesses into work for the parishes. In Holland there has been a special commission appointed by the union which federates most of the deaconess houses in the country to survey the question of deaconess training; and with the approval of this commission the deaconess house in Utrecht started a special class to train parish sisters (social workers). Later a branch house was opened to specialise in this training, omitting nursing from the curriculum. This is an example of the third of the types of deaconess work mentioned in the opening paragraphs, appearing within the context of a deaconess mother house. The Austrian report comments that deaconesses who enter parish work as parish sisters find themselves in a very difficult position. Because of the shortage of staff they have to teach women and children in Bible study and services, perhaps also to teach religion in the day school, and at the same time to carry on the charitable work of the parish, a very heavy task in post-war conditions. So among these parish sisters some feel a sense of strain in trying to do anything beyond charitable work, while others are irked by the restriction which the charitable work, by the time it takes up, puts on their desire to evangelise. The report says that the lack of recruits for deaconess work is most noticeable in this field, but as nearly every other report says that it is in this work that the demand is greatest it may be a relative rather than an absolute shortage. Nevertheless the point is well made that those deaconesses who turn to parish work in the sense of evangelistic and teaching work cannot also do social work.

Along with an increasing trend towards parish-centred deaconess work there not unnaturally goes a desire for some redefinition of the relationship of the deaconess orders to the Church, and of the individual deaconess to the parish for which she is working. Normally a deaconess is consecrated to the work of her order. The Dutch report puts the matter well in saying that consecration often takes place *in* a church but not *by* the Church. In Sweden the consecration of a deaconess is by the Bishop and takes place in church, a form of service appearing in the church manual; but she is not ordained. The manager of deaconess institutions in Sweden has to be a clergyman. Often in other countries the strongest link between the deaconess order and the Church is the presidency of a minister over the board or the joint rule of a chaplain and the matron or head in the mother house. In Holland there has been appointed a Council of the Church 'for the church and the care of the sick', intended to be the link between the Church and the deaconess houses. 'Otherwise,' says the report, 'there are no official relations with the Church' except in the missions overseas, which have become a part of the Church so that their personnel, including deaconesses, are now the servants of the Church. The Swiss report makes a strong plea that the deaconess who comes to work in a parish should be dedicated to the work in church and clearly identified in the eyes of the people as the agent of the Church.

The second type of deaconess is the Anglican. In 1862 Elizabeth Ferard was made a deaconess in the Anglican Church by the Bishop of London. She was a woman of vision and energy. Her main contention was that the pastoral work of a big city parish was far too heavy to be borne by the clergy alone. With six other women she founded the London Deaconess Institution to train deaconesses. Other institutions grew up in other dioceses: most of them are now obsolete, training being concentrated in a few centres. Anglican deaconesses are not trained as nurses; their training is mainly theological and pastoral. In their particular sphere of work they are not under the discipline of the house in which they were trained, i.e. the idea of mother houses does not exist. They wear uniform. Each deaconess is responsible to the Bishop of the diocese in which she works. The Bishop usually appoints a Head Deaconess, but she exercises no authority over the others. There grew up within the London Institution (now obsolete) a community of deaconesses, still very active, called the Deaconess Community of S. Andrew, all the members of which are fully professed Sisters, wearing the habit and taking the Vows of Religion.[1]

In 1920 the Lambeth Conference (the ten-yearly meeting of all the Bishops of the Anglican Communion throughout the world) recommended the revival of the Diaconate of Women in the Church, and the appropriate bodies in England, the Convocations of Canterbury and York (the supreme authority in matters of Faith and Order in the Church of England) took action in the years 1923 and 1925 respectively. Further resolutions in these bodies decided upon the status and function of the deaconesses. By resolution of Convocation 'the Order of Deaconesses is the one existing ordained ministry for women, in the sense of being the only Order of Ministry in the Anglican Communion to which women are admitted by episcopal imposition of hands'. Canons in the new Canon Law now before Convocation concern the office of deaconess. The deaconess dedicates herself to lifelong service but takes no vows. The extremely careful report of the Archbishops' Committee on the ministry of women (1919) makes it clear that those who worked for the re-establishment of the Order of Deaconesses were concerned with their status within church order, wanting to provide for women a place hitherto lacking in the permanent ministry of the Church.

There are some three hundred deaconesses in the Church of England. They work in parishes at home and overseas and some of them teach in schools. One deaconess teaching in a school exercised a great influence throughout her diocese, teaching and lecturing to clergy and laity. A woman who wishes to become a deaconess must first train as a lay church worker (two years) before she can be considered by a Selection Board and, if accepted, proceed to the additional training required for a deaconess. The deaconess is highly trained theologically: the New Zealand report says she has 'the same training as a male candidate for the ministry'.

[1] See p. 116.

The Anglican Churches in Canada, Australia and New Zealand train and ordain deaconesses. The Anglican Church in South Africa had deaconesses from England, one of whom has trained an African woman, now ordained by her bishop. It might seem that the revival of the Order of Deaconesses has stabilised the position in the Church of England in regard to the ordination of women, and provided them with a form of service suited to women's gifts. Yet difficulties and anomalies remain. Thus in the Church Assembly, which is the legislative and administrative body charged with the practical working of the Church of England except in matters of Faith and Order, many women have a place, but no deaconesses, for to sit as lay women would compromise their position, and they are not allowed to sit as clergy. Deaconesses may, with episcopal permission, read the statutory services of Morning and Evening Prayer, and preach at non-liturgical services and administer the chalice at the Holy Communion, but in point of fact seldom do. There are also in the Church of England lay readers, men who are licensed by the bishops to read services, preach and administer the chalice in Holy Communion in understaffed parishes. They need not have any theological qualifications. Women are not allowed to be lay readers, one of the arguments against this being that if they were, nothing distinctive would remain which deaconesses were allowed to do by virtue of their ordination and others were not. The New Zealand report comments that the very slow recruitment of women to the order of deaconesses (there are only nine) may, at least in part, be due to the fact that 'some suitable women have not felt attracted to ordination because it did not offer to them any more opportunities for service than were open to them without it'. Much more use could be made of these very highly trained women if only there were not so rooted a conviction in the Churches that the proper place for women's work is the poor parish and the poor only. University students, women with a secondary school education—these need pastoral care as much as others and the deaconess is trained to give it. The difficulty is that so many clergy are so overburdened with the routine of conducting services, marrying and burying, that they would rather have the most slenderly qualified curate who can take some of this off their shoulders than the trained and experienced deaconess who is not allowed to.

The third type of deaconess, common to Presbyterian, Baptist and Methodist churches, lies between the first two, approximating more nearly to the second than to the first in that these deaconesses work directly under the churches they serve, as distinct from belonging to mother houses. Most of them do not, however, like the Anglicans make a lifelong profession. The main difference is that in those Churches which have them they are the *only* type of full-time paid worker of recognised status and training, and range widely in the work they do from parish work to institutional work in orphanages, homes for the aged, and other church-supported institutions. Many are already nurses or social workers when they offer their services. In some communions a different name appears to be used in different countries—thus while the Presbyterian Church in New Zealand and Australia has orders of deaconesses, the corresponding women workers in the Presbyterian Church of England are called church sisters. After two years' work they may be ordained as elders, but are not thereby made members of the Session, i.e. the ordination gives them the status of elders without the function.

The order of deaconesses in the Methodist Church was revived in 1880. There are about 220 Methodist deaconesses at work in England, and some 30 in the foreign mission fields of the Methodist Church. The Methodist Church in the United States has approximately 565 deaconesses in active work, about a quarter of them are in parochial work, some in inter-denominational work of different kinds, and a considerable number in hospitals and other church institutions (from this it would seem that some at least of the American Methodist deaconesses have nursing training, though this is not specified in the report).

In the Church of Scotland there were, when the survey was made, both deaconesses (43) and church sisters (115). The Order of Deaconesses was restored in the Church of Scotland in 1888. The first deaconess was set apart by the kirk session of Bowden. Deaconesses held posts as heads of educational institutions, and are engaged in organising and administrative work. There was, however, so much overlap between the deaconess and the church sister in the parish that for a time deaconesses were not being recruited for parish work, and the service and status of women workers was reviewed by a committee, which reported to the General Assembly. In 1949 the Assembly recommended that all church sisters should be 'commissioned and set apart as deaconesses'. The question of allowing them more scope is under discussion. They are given a two-year training at the women's missionary college, St. Colm's, directed especially towards parish work. They are selected by and work under the Women's Home Mission Committee of the Home Board of the Church. The work is pastoral and social. A particularly interesting piece of work is done among the girls of the herring fleet, the deaconesses going with them from the far North down the coast of England as they follow the moving herring shoals.

The Baptist Churches of Great Britain also have an order of deaconesses working directly under the Baptist Assembly. Their training and their work approximate very closely to that of the Methodist deaconesses. In Sweden the deaconesses of the Baptist Church are nearly all nurses and do social work under the church authorities.

It is interesting to note that in South Africa the Presbyterian and the Methodist Churches have tried to establish deaconess orders but without success. The Methodists have deaconesses working in Johannesburg and along the Reef (Transvaal), trained in England and supported by the Deaconess Society of Transvaal. In 1945 Conference in South Africa (the highest authority in Methodism) decided that there should be an Order of Deaconesses throughout South Africa, and provision was made for their training. A wide appeal for recruits was fruitless, partly because there are openings in social work for the same type of candidate, partly because of the difficulty that most of the people among whom the work would be done are Afrikaans-speaking girls and women who have come into the towns from the countryside in recent years. The Presbyterian Church also has only succeeded in re-cruiting one full and two part-time deaconesses. The Dutch Reformed Church has no deaconesses, but its large band of social workers do in many cases much the same work. The Congrega-tionalists, who do not have deaconesses or church sisters in Great Britain or among the European population, in South Africa have a number of African workers, trained at the Lovedale Mission School, carrying on all sorts of social and evangelistic work.

Some of the same difficulties arise in these orders of deaconesses, and their relation to their Churches, as arise in the Church of

England. The Methodist deaconesses, although they are ordained women, find themselves placed among lay representatives to Conference, the highest court of the Church. They are not free to administer the Sacrament, although occasional dispensation to do so has been given to deaconesses in exceptional circumstances. The tradition of lay preaching is so strong in the Methodist Church that there are no difficulties for deaconesses on that score. Deaconesses have often exercised a full pastoral ministry including administration of the Sacraments, in churches too small and poor for a minister, and in new areas such as housing estates. This is reported by, among others, the English Baptists and by the Reformed Church in Austria. A number of examples of work of this kind done by deaconesses for congregations left without pastors in the war are given in the German report. The Methodists in Argentina, where there are one-sixth as many deaconesses as pastors, report that many deaconesses 'are really doing all the work of a pastor except administer the Sacraments'.

OTHER TYPES OF WOMEN WORKERS IN THE PARISH AND CONGREGATION

Trained lay parish workers. A number of Churches have, by careful experiment over a period of years, worked out a system of recruiting and training women for work in the parishes on a full-time salaried basis. Their duties vary with the type of parish, and the degree of responsibility they are given depends on the minister and the parish council. Sunday School and Youth work, Bible study in groups, preparation for Confirmation, home visiting, hospital visiting, especially in maternity hospitals, club work for women, girls and old people, social case work, especially if the district needs it and she is qualified—any or all of these tasks may fall to the parish worker. She does not do nursing. Her work in a new housing area can be of quite incalculable value. Often she moves in with the first tenants, living in a room in one of the houses, and she is there to give every kind of help to people who do not know each other, to whom the life of having a house of their own is strange, and who have a thousand and one problems which need friendly help. For the most part women workers are not compelled to wear distinctive dress, though in practice they often find it useful to do so.

The Church of England has been developing the training of lay women parish workers for many years and has a number of training establishments. Some of these colleges also train deaconesses, for whom the first two years of training is the same as that of a lay worker. Two years residential training is insisted upon—residence is important for girls who have never been away from home and now have to work in a job where personal relationships count for much. After training a woman is licensed by a bishop to work in a particular parish in his diocese, under the minister and church council. The whole work is under the guidance of the Central Council for Women's Church Work (appointed by and responsible to the Church Assembly) which has established a definite standard in the inter-diocesan certificate and also selects workers. Some 50 or 60 new licences are granted annually. The Church Army and the Ranyard Mission also train women for parish work: they are of a lower educational standard and do very fine work in poor parishes. Most dioceses now have Boards of Women's Work, composed of voluntary persons with a paid secretary. They look after recruitment, help to pay for training, see to placing, and play an important part in being always there to help the worker. The Protestant Episcopal Church of America has some 3,000 full-time women church workers, some in parish work but most of them in church institutions as nurses, social workers and secretaries. The Church demands of workers 'a year of graduate study including "religious content" material and some professional specialised training'. The average length of training is two years in most American Churches.

In Switzerland there are also parish workers, about 65 being at work in different cantons. The parish worker is trained at the Zurich Social School, where a two-year course in social work is followed by a six-months' course in preparation for parish work. She works with women and girls, especailly in club work, and much of her time is taken up with visiting, often dealing with officials about the needs of parishioners. She does not do any teaching except in emergency, and a good deal of secretarial work in the parish, looking after the parish notice board and organising the delivery of magazines falls to her lot—tasks which in many other countries would be considered the proper affair of volunteers, (this report elsewhere comments that not enough is done by the laity of some parishes and that they need leadership). The Swiss parish workers are joined together in a professional society and have a magazine of their own.

This seems the right place to mention a piece of work in Zurich which, although it is organised by volunteers, is also connected with the parish helpers. This is the Churches' Centre of Parish Work. The place is in a sense a settlement, a large building with a resident head and a large staff of voluntary and a few paid helpers. The task of the centre is mostly family case work, and ministers send to the centre the cases needing help—admission to hospital or homes, help in getting pensions and so on. The centre looks after travellers of all kinds, innumerable immigrants, tramps off the roads, unemployed and broken down folk. A dozen seamstresses work full-time making over old clothes, patching up the poor, doing paid work to help out the budget. Help is given to women incapable of running their households and they are taught and helped by volunteers. This centre is also a sort of mother house to church and social workers of all kinds and arranges conferences and refresher courses for them.

Parish Helpers (as they are called) in Germany fulfil much the same tasks as have been described elsewhere. 'Most of the larger parishes, especially in the towns, employ them,' says the report. They receive two years training at a Bible school, eighteen months of study and six months of practical work under supervision. The largest Bible school, the Burchardthaus, sends out about 60 trained women each year and the average annual output by all the schools is estimated at 200–250 in the report, which comments that many of the girls come from parsonage homes. The salary is about equal to that of a shorthand typist.

In France it is not easy to distinguish between different types of church worker. Of a total of fifty or so working in the French Reformed Church seventeen are in posts recognised by the Church, and thirty-three in posts not officially recognised. There is as yet no regulation of their training, or of their position in the Church. A Commission was appointed in 1950 to examine the work of parish assistants and draw up a statute regulating their position. Some of these parish assistants have had a theological training, others have been secretaries or organisers in Youth movements, some have a State nursing certificate, others have a teaching diploma. Many are women who have made themselves useful to their own pastors and have attained the place of assistant.

The Reformed Church in France is, for the most part, a scattered one: pastors often do not know the part of the country in which they minister, and a woman who knows the locality is often preferred to a trained outsider. The work of parish assistants varies very much. While some of them have a piece of the work of the parish under their control, so that they can develop it as their own special responsibility, or may be in charge, practically speaking, of a distant sub-congregation which the pastor can only reach occasionally, others are expected to lend a hand in a general way and have no responsibilities of their own. Their salaries are very low and the writer of the report remarks that although the woman who is fortunate in her pastor may be able to do useful and satisfying work, for the most part 'the woman who could be a nurse, a welfare worker or a teacher is committing a folly, from a sheerly practical point of view in becoming a church worker'. Honest speaking. But something is being done to help overcome the loneliness of these workers and to bring them into touch with other Christian workers, such as youth leaders and the women leaders in Cimade and the deaconesses. Conferences have been arranged for them, and they have a magazine.

Outside Europe and the United States, mention ought to be made of the promising development of women's work in Argentina and Uruguay. The Union Theological Seminary, Buenos Aires (Methodist, Presbyterian, Disciples of Christ and Waldensian) trains men for the ministries of these Churches and also accepts women for theological training. A number of these women are going to marry ministers and take a theological course in order to be able to help their husbands. Recently the training school for Christian Women Workers has merged with the Seminary. Two courses are available to a woman, one of university level, basically the same as that of men candidates for the ministry, with different specialisations to fit her for work as a deaconess or church worker with special charge of an outlying congregation in a Methodist circuit, or work as a missionary, nurse or educationist. This is a six-year course, and one year of practical experience must be gained before the last two years of study are entered upon. The other course is adapted for girls who left school early and in later years decided that they wished to do church work; it is a five-year course with a year's practice before the last year. The

Argentina report comments that it is only the steady raising of the standard of girls' education over the past years that has made possible this work by women with a broader educational background.

In Manchuria, before the country was occupied by the Japanese, women were admitted on equal terms with men for theological education and could also take a special course qualifying them to work as Church sisters. Manchuria was occupied by the Japanese longer than any other country and the people suffered terribly during the occupation. Coal and food were taken from the people and used elsewhere, and in the bitter winters doctors and nurses worked with frozen hands in the wards and operating theatres of the church hospitals, of which the country had thirteen. The Church in Manchuria (a separate Synod of the Church of Christ in China) has been richly blessed in the women who have thrown up successful careers and taken theological training, and then worked in the congregation or have gone out to the villages, travelling around preaching and helping. 'They sometimes do all the work of a pastor except administer the Sacraments. Others have been responsible for superintending the work of the Church in a whole district, travelling round, staying in one place for several weeks, organising women's meetings and preparing candidates for baptism.' Of a lower grade of training are the church sisters, who usually work in one place. When foreign missionaries were interned or withdrawn, the women of the Church took over their work, travelling about the districts into which the Church is divided, holding evangelistic meetings and Bible schools, keeping up the work of home visiting and the Sunday Schools. 'In the state of the country in war conditions this called for great courage. In the Japanese-controlled Church there was little place for women leaders in the scheme of things. Senior and junior women evangelists alike were constantly questioned and ill-treated by the special police. All religious meetings were suspect. The police followed evangelists and church sisters on their visits to the homes of church members or non-members, sat through their talks and listened to all that was said, or demanded that the full report of an address should be handed in to the police station. Owing to the poverty of the country salaries grew less and less, but the women stuck to their jobs until they were literally starved out and their clothing in rags.'

The American Mission Bible Training School in Egypt prepares women by a three-year course to do evangelistic work among other women. Although in Mohammedan countries women are less rigidly confined to their homes than they were, the main way of reaching them is by house visiting. The level of literacy among women is still very low, so that unless reading is taught Bibles and Christian literature are not much use. The women turned out by this Bible school are sometimes supported by the mission, or by the church or by both. 'Girls with full High School training often carry on this work even though the public still looks rather askance at girls who go from house to house and who hold public meetings. Girls from other missions are sent to this school and Coptic girls also attend.' The American Mission alone employs 47 of these young trained women, and the total in Egypt is between 70 and 80. Between them the 47 Bible teachers of the American Mission teach some 7,000 women a year in their homes. Club work for girls in towns and villages, visiting, and teaching church women to read and play a proper part in church life are also parts of the work of these Bible teachers.

It is interesting to note that Norway, Sweden and Denmark do not report the existence of trained parish workers of any kind, except the deaconesses. The Swedish report definitely says that there are 'very few paid posts for women in the Church, those that exist being for a few youth organisers and travelling missionary secretaries'. Norway reports one woman worker recently sent to work among industrial workers.

SPECIALISED WORK OF WOMEN FOR THE CHURCHES

The parish worker combines an immense number of functions. In a rather small parish she has to be both a social worker and an evangelist: or she may find that she is mostly an administrative factotum, secretary to the minister and odd-job-man. In the very big parish, still more in the region or grouping of churches there is room for the specialist who, by her training and experience, is able to help both the all-round parish worker and the volunteer. Some of these specialists are chiefly concerned with religious education, others with social work. As with deaconesses and lay workers, so with the specialists, it is not possible to draw very clear lines, and a number of omissions are bound to occur.

Directors of Religious Education. This title and office seem to be unique to the American Churches. Many of the functions of directors of education are performed in other congregations if not by the minister himself by the women workers in the parishes, and by volunteers. Not all religious education directors are women—about two-thirds are, but in a recent survey of the work by Dr. Shaver, who on behalf of the Congregational Christian Churches took particulars of the work in most denominations, two-thirds of the pastors he approached would have preferred men if they could have been obtained.

The history of the religious education director has been an unhappy one. The idea was taken up with some enthusiasm and a number of Bible schools and a few theological seminaries trained women for the work. Soon there were no posts for them. Now the difficulty is the reverse and denominational agencies which attempt to act as employment bureaus cannot find enough women for the work. Unfortunately, many Churches have taken to employing young women with very little training who can be had for very small salaries. The religious education director has no status in the Church as a whole, her security is almost non-existent, with the result that the average time that a woman stays in one church is as low as two years—hardly adequate for making a dint on a situation. The directors themselves in answering questions say that what they chiefly lack is training in the technique of teaching and in managing human relations. The task is often a large and amorphous one, planning the education of adults and children, a task for which 'training on the job' by the busy pastor is quite inadequate. Only a very tiny percentage of the women at present working in theological colleges wanted to become directors of religious education.

In the Church of England there are religious education organisers attached to many dioceses. Their job is to travel round helping local churches, to organise and on occasion give courses of lectures. They often are the contact between the church and the State schools. Some of these organisers are women.

Trained Youth Leaders. Specially trained leaders of youth work are a comparatively recent development in the churches. Gone are the days when anyone who 'liked young people' or wanted to influence them for good could lead a club. The chief reason why the

Churches have had to take the training of youth leaders seriously is the competition of secular clubs, run by political parties, by co-operatives, by education authorities, by industrial firms and even by cinemas. Very often the trained youth leader is drawn from one or other of the classes of worker already mentioned, and takes a special course of training for youth work after discovering a special bent for it. The difficulty in training specialists in this field, who are not also general church workers, is that few youth leaders can stay at the job till they die or retire, and probably none should! Since youth leaders are both men and women this is hardly the place for a detailed discussion of what they do.

Church Social Workers. This is a very confusing term. In society at large the term 'social work' can perhaps mean something, but in the Church no woman is engaged purely on social work, for she works as a Church social worker rather than a State social worker because she believes that all social problems have a religious aspect and some of them a religious cause and cure. The term refers largely to the kind of training she has had, which may enable her to make her approach to religious questions through the care of people's bodies, through nursing, psychiatric work, family case work, work for the deaf, dumb and blind.

The main types of social work still performed within a parish are nursing and family case work. Often these tasks are performed by deaconesses (in those countries where there are deaconesses of the German type). Family case work, usual in industrial areas or large cities, needs expert care, and the social worker usually hands on the cases to suitable agencies for further care. A few churches have clinics on their premises (one is mentioned in the report from Argentina in a church where there is a woman minister). Some churches run crèches for the children of working mothers, and the Danish report speaks of kindergartens—some 40 or so in different parts of the country—run by separate congregations. But for the most part social work becomes steadily more and more specialised: physical and mental handicaps of all kinds, psychological conditions—all these need medical skill and they need specialised institutions. An immense amount of human suffering and incapacity which used to be looked on as irremediable now can be cured, but the cure is costly, far beyond the resources of congregations or even of whole Churches. The result is that institutions originally financed and governed entirely by the Church now either receive large grants from public authorities and conform to conditions of recruitment, training and terms of employment, or are passing steadily from the control of church bodies to the control of public bodies. The American report remarks that social workers employed by large church institutions 'scarcely think of themselves as church workers' and that church institutions, more especially hospitals, are passing to public control.

There are, however, several kinds of social work which remain in the hands of the Churches and of Christian bodies created by them. These are for the most part types of work which are best done by small institutions and which do not demand the services of highly trained specialists or elaborate equipment. In the care of young children modern teaching based on psychological studies emphasises the small group with varieties in age as the best type of life for the child with no normal home. There has also been a strong reaction against putting old people into hospitals when there is no one to care for them and against treating them as sick when they show the symptoms of a healthy old age. Even in countries where hospitals and schools are passing rapidly to the State, children's homes remain under Christian bodies, and the concern of the Churches for old people is increasing.

Certain specialised kinds of social service also remain in the hands of the Churches. There is always room for experiment to meet new social needs as they arise. Thus the Society of Friends in Great Britain has recently undertaken work with problem families —those in which squalor and undiscipline persist in spite of re-housing and every form of public help having been tried. Many Churches faced by the large number of marriages which break down have started Marriage Guidance, including both case work for couples who are drifting towards separation, and educational work. Voluntary helpers are trained for this work, though they must already be doctors, social workers or in some other way suited to give such help. Churches still undertake social work where moral as well as physical reclamation is needed. Josephine Butler, more than any other woman, revolutionised the average nineteenth century attitude to illegitimacy. Hitherto the blame was laid at the door of the mother, and she and her child were made to suffer. Her work led not only to the founding of the Girls'

Friendly Societies known today in Great Britain and on the continent, but to special training for moral welfare work. In every country where it operates—and it is remarkably spread throughout the world—the women officers of the Salvation Army carry on social work, some of it demanding very special skill. The officers in charge of this work would probably insist that they are evangelists, as indeed they are, and more often than not the specialisation is due to the fact that a particular woman has certain marked gifts rather than to any highly diversified training. Hostels and shelters for the destitute, homes for unmarried mothers and their children, old people's homes, work at the police courts and prisons, work with delinquents, family case work with extremely difficult families, training for mothers convicted of cruelty to their children—all these are types of work carried out by the Salvation Army, whose mission has always been centred upon those whom the middle-class churches could not touch.

Sunday School Organisers. For thousands of women in the Churches the only training they have ever received is a course of study and practical demonstration of methods in a conference or course on Sunday School work. The trained Sunday School organiser is usually attached to a regional group of churches such as an Anglican diocese, or she is employed by a Sunday School Association. Her main work is to go round the Sunday Schools in her area and to organise courses and conferences for teachers. If she is on the headquarters staff she takes a hand in the preparation of courses of lessons or may edit a magazine for teachers. Some Sunday School organisers are trained teachers, and in most countries some special training for the work is required.

OTHER SERVICES OF WOMEN TO THE CHURCH

At the end of this section of the reports are grouped together, somewhat incongruously sometimes, the different professional offices held by women in the Churches. There are many women it appears who are church organists, paid for their work; some Churches reckon that as many as a third of their organists are women, many of whom are also in charge of and train the choir. Religious journalism also seems to be a field in which many women work, both as contributors, and as editors. Of the writing of books by women there is no end, especially in the field of religious education, though their contribution to theological studies is very small. Holland has a distinguished woman theologian at the head of a Protestant broadcasting system. The legal adviser to the Evangelical Church in Germany is a woman. There are some women architects who have designed churches or church buildings, but these are few. One of the best known artists in Greece today is a woman who has revived the ancient art of mosaic with very great success.

Women Foreign Missionaries. With the exception of the deaconesses in Germany, and the large ill-defined body of women who do social work through church institutions of which it is impossible to obtain numbers, women missionaries are the largest category of women in the full-time service of the Church. They outnumber trained workers in the parishes in almost every country. How long this is likely to be so, with the closing of foreign mission fields, no one knows. Foreign missionary work gave women their first chance of showing what services they could render to the Church, and in spite of the opening of many doors for full-time work for the Churches at home, it is still true in very many Churches that the woman with gifts, vision and a great will for service finds all her powers more fully exercised abroad than at home. The main spheres of missionary work vary very little between country and country: education, medical work and district evangelism being the main work.

The central concern of this book is not with the missionary societies as such, but with the Churches out of which they grew and the Churches they have planted all over the world. Another book could be written about the place of women in the missionary movement in the past 150 years and today and the effect they have had on the development of that movement, which would never have been the same without them. Nor would the Churches that now exist all over the world be what they are if the Gospel had been taken to these lands by men only, or by men accompanied by their wives. In so far as Christianity has struck its roots deep into the lives of the people of Africa and the East, it has done so because the women of those countries have been reached. For, in so many cases it was the women who had most to receive from the Gospel, the heaviest chains to lose, and, at the same time, often the highest price to pay for the new freedom because of the binding power of custom on the woman, and her helplessness in her complete dependence on men. 'Breaking away from religious affiliations in our country is not an easy thing,' writes an Indian woman. 'It involves persecution, social ostracism and humiliation. This is because the religions of the country are of a socio-religious nature and in this milieu every social and personal activity is carried out, even eating and drinking. Therefore it is an act of very great courage on the part of one accepting Christianity to adjust herself to other ways, both in religious outlook and ways of living, whether the convert is a new one or one made two generations ago.' The main task of the woman missionary has therefore been to make a new life for women converts, and this has most often been done through the creation of institutions, especially schools and colleges in which the atmosphere of a Christian family or fellowship prevailed. Several of the letters from Indian Christian women say that in these institutions for women something more has been achieved than the handing out of a largely western form of education. There has been real concern for the development of personality, and the drive to sacrifice everything else to the gaining of paper qualifications which will lead to a well paid job has been more successfully resisted in girls' than in boys' education. The social result of the Christian education of girls and women has been, says one Indian writer, 'very significant, for it has helped to eliminate a number of social evils, for example, the age of marriage is raised, there are fewer child wives and child widows, there are more love marriages as against the marriages arranged by parents and relatives'. This work in Christian institutions has been for many years not wholly or even chiefly the work of the foreign missionary alone. Very large numbers of missionary institutions, both schools and colleges, hospitals and training schools for nurses have been under the leadership of the women of the country, and the foreign missionary has often fitted happily into a pattern of which she was no longer the keystone. This has meant that the older type of woman missionary, who had to be a tough character and an individualist if she was to stand loneliness and the isolation, both from her own male colleagues and from the people of the country who regarded an unmarried as an unmarriageable woman, has gradually to be replaced by the type of woman who, still a person of character, is primarily a co-operator, rather than an individualist.

This leads to another question, touched upon earlier. In many countries the institutions built by Christian missions are passing into the hands of the secular State, or are being subjected to increasing pressure from the State. Sometimes, notably in the Near East, this pressure amounts to a severe infringement of religious liberty. In China, where there has been the greatest concentration of missionary personnel and funds, no one knows for how long Christian institutions will be able to maintain their Christian character: already China is returning to that inaccessibility to foreign missionary work which was her condition for centuries. It may very well be that the future of Christianity in that country and in others in like condition may turn on whether or not it is preserved in the homes of the people. In other words, what will be tested is largely what the women have done, what seed they have sown among the women for whom they worked, how tenacious the faith of the mothers who, with every school secularised, may be the sole educators of the young in the Christian faith. The single woman missionary has always been at a great disadvantage in working for the creation of Christian homes. In an institution her habits of life would be known to all and she had a chance of making it something of a home for those who worked with her. But as an evangelist working in the villages among women all of whom were married, or about to be married, whose social customs were such that they found it impossible to believe in the possibility of an unmarried woman being chaste, she was at a very great disadvantage in trying to teach the principles of Christian home life. The unmarried woman, Chinese, Indian or African, would be under an equal handicap. The married woman missionary, on the other hand, was often too tied by her own children to give time to mission work, and might be out of the country for long periods while her children were being educated. If childless, she would probably be regarded as under a curse. In spite of these drawbacks, much has been done. The doctor and the nurse have an immediate entry to the hearts of women through help given in sickness and childbirth, and this help has often been the first overleaping of the barrier. But the building of Christian home life is the work of years of patient education. Women are not only, when Christian, the pillars of the faith, but when halfchristianised they are the preservers of superstition. The building of Christian home life is now increasingly occupying the minds of Churches and missions. It means for the woman missionary a closer co-operation with the men workers in the same area, to ensure that the Christian message is presented to families and not to individuals, and it means closer working with the Church, and with the married women within the Church who have to be helped to see that they are the ones on whom the responsibility ultimately rests.

In the Churches of the countries which sent them out, women missionaries have had an immense influence, far exceeding the personal influence of one or two outstanding missionaries who have by their words persuaded others to take up the same work. The missionaries were the first class of women (again with the exception of the German deaconesses) to be specially trained for their jobs. For men deciding to go abroad as missionaries, it has almost always been considered by missionary societies sufficient, if they were ordained, that a few missionary talks should be introduced into the ordination course. Most missionary societies insist on some special residential training for women, even for doctors, nurses and teachers who have qualified professionally. These missionary training colleges, some of them joint institutions of several societies, have done a remarkable work in training women whose sole qualifications for the work they wanted to undertake were willingness and character. These colleges have had an unquestioned influence on the development of training for women in other kinds of church work. One interesting development in the training of missionaries is mentioned in the British report. A woman[1] who had spent many years as principal of a training college for women missionaries, retired from the work, and with a small band of supporters bought a house in the country and ultimately a farm, where a small number of women, all one-time missionaries, made a community with a simple discipline, and received as guests church workers and missionaries home from the field. Their chief aim was, however, to cope with a problem becoming more and more pressing, the high proportion of single women missionaries suffering from physical and nervous breakdowns or in other ways finding themselves incapable of carrying on the work beyond the first few years. (This point

[1] See *Florence Allshorn* by J. H. Oldham. S.C.M. Press.

receives corroboration from the French report which says that
foreign mission work is almost the only idea of the young woman
who wants to serve Christ: many go into it who ought to be in
some less exacting field, and are broken by the strain.) The aim of
the St. Julian's community is to help those who have broken
down in these ways to recover, and to prevent similar failure by
bringing the young woman missionary at home on her first
furlough into the house or the farm where she works with others,
is helped by the spiritual life of the place, and, in particular, learns
that the besetting sin of the single woman in a tropical climate is
too fierce and earnest a concentration on her work, to the exclusion of spending time on making a home for herself and her
colleagues, and exemplifying in the community life of the mission
station that Christian community which the members so often
preach. This has been the conspicuous failure of many mission
stations, that they often consist of individuals going their own
way even in open criticism of each other. It is the single women
who suffer most from the lack of a genuine community life, and a
feverish concentration on work, forms, timetables, and a ceaseless
routine is often an attempt to stifle the sense of a failure in living.
For the woman on the foreign mission field the occasional escapes
and diversions of the parish worker at home are not available: if
she cannot make a life of friendship with her colleagues of whatever race, and of gracious living in which the worker does not
kill the woman, she seldom has any other means of becoming a
mature person. The St. Julian's community is a revolt against the
idea of a too academic training of women at the expense of training to live as a person in fellowship with others—the most
powerful form of Christian witness. It is also a revolt against the
idea that training can ever be successfully completed in young
persons, and before they have the experience of knowing in their
work what it is that they still lack; the community, like the post-
war 'Church and World' institute in Holland, emphasises the
importance of a period of training after a spell of work.

As well as influencing the conception of training women for
church work, women missionaries have had a great influence on
the status of women in the churches. 'The women missionaries,' says
the Swedish report, 'are the only women—beside the deaconesses
—who are allowed consecration for the office by the Church. A
bishop generally performs the ceremony of missionary consecra-

tion and in the service book of the Church of Sweden the rules are the same for women as for men.' This consecration of women missionaries in the Swedish Church is mentioned in the South African report, the women of the Churches in South Africa having noted the practice from Swedish missionaries at work there. The Swedish Baptists mention that not only were returning missionaries the first women to speak in churches, but that they were completely accepted although there was strong opposition to the idea of women at home preaching or speaking in churches. The Norwegian report mentions that women on the mission field are forced by circumstances to accept the responsibilities that come their way and that what they have done is often held up as an example of what women can do for the Church if they are allowed the chance. The Dutch report, on the other hand, says that 'on the whole, women have not held a very prominent place in the mission field. Teachers and nurses are not called missionaries in our country, but are considered to be auxiliary workers. The name missionary is only applied to those with a full theological training doing evangelistic work'. Missionary training for auxiliary workers only began after the war, consisting at first of a course of a few days. Later a six months' course for auxiliaries and missionaries' wives (to whose work a very warm tribute is paid in the report) was held with great success. The women who have theological qualifications and work as evangelists in Indonesia hold subordinate positions in the missions.

It cannot be said that the regard in which the woman missionary is held by the home Churches has resulted in any considerable number of appointments of women to the home boards of foreign missionary societies. Unless, as in some cases, separate women's boards send out women missionaries, the proportion of women on home boards, although increasing, does not equal the proportion of women on the mission field.

Foreign missionary activity is no longer an activity only of Western Churches (indeed there are some Western Churches which because of their political situation have no foreign mission work, such as the Church of Czechoslovakia and the Reformed Church of Hungary). Churches which a hundred years ago, or even less, did not exist, now carry on foreign missionary work of their own. Mention has already been made of the work of the National Missionary Society of India, which is foreign in the sense that the missionaries are hundreds of miles from home and in a different language area, although they may not have left the sub-continent of India. The Burmese Churches send missionaries to remote valleys, to tribes speaking another language who are primitive animists. The Korean Churches before 1940 supported four missionaries and two teachers in Manchuria and three women missionaries in China. (The Japanese forbade the Women's Missionary Society to continue as a national organisation and allowed only local women's meetings.) From Egypt women have gone to the Sudan (probably about twenty, says the report). It is fairly certain that these are not the only instances although they are the main ones mentioned in the reports.

The Biblewoman and her modern counterpart. One of the main tasks of the woman missionary engaged in evangelistic rather than in institutional work was the training of Biblewomen. The Biblewoman seems to be known, and by that name, in every mission from China to South America. The task of the Biblewoman was to receive some simple training from the woman missionary in Bible teaching and then to go visiting in the homes of the people in towns and villages, teaching the women to read, telling them Bible stories and praying with them. In nearly all non-Christian cultures the only women who are able to do this work are widows: they were the only women who were free and they were the only ones who would be accepted in the homes. Many of them had very harsh experiences in former days. Some of these women, if they were filled with a real love of souls and had some innate teaching ability, did do very fine work, but as the general educational level of the communities in which they worked began to rise (especially in the cities), it became clear that many of them were only partially effective, that some merely repeated by rote what the missionary had said. A further difficulty tended to arise from the fact that they were under the exclusive charge of the woman missionary. If she were not *persona grata* in the Church, neither were they. Their very existence tended sometimes to cause the women of a church to say that evangelism was 'Biblewomen's work', and not only to excuse themselves from it on these grounds but to despise it as a lowly occupation.

One remedy for this situation is to recruit a different type of woman worker to replace the Biblewoman and to train her more adequately. The successful work on these lines of the American Mission in Egypt is described in the section headed Parish Workers. These young, single, better-educated women take the place of the Biblewomen. Their work is still mainly house to house visiting, though club work is added to it.

In the South African report an interesting development is described. The Women's Auxiliary of the Methodist Church supports nearly sixty African Biblewomen who work in the locations among African women. A woman with some vision gave a sum of money during the war for running an experimental training course for these Biblewomen. Twenty Methodist and one Presbyterian Biblewomen were sent to the Lovedale Bible School, a missionary institution of Scottish origin, for a three-months' course. It included Bible study, pastoralia, preparation of addresses, Sunday School work, some first aid and health teaching and plenty of opportunity for discussion in groups under skilled leadership. The Biblewoman also did some hospital visiting, and evangelistic and Sunday School work in neighbouring villages. 'There is no doubt at all,' says the report, 'of the profound impression left on the women who attended. In many cases it has been a revolutionary spiritual experience.' A gift from Scotland enabled a hostel to be built at Lovedale, and an instructress has been appointed for future courses. She also travels round and visits the Biblewomen at their work, giving short local courses attended by women of all denominations. The following year twelve women were given a five months' course.

The Burmese report contains a paragraph which might well be put on the title page of this book to indicate the difference in *ethos* between the settled congregations of Europe and America and the still fluid situation in countries where Christianity is only a hundred years old. 'It has been a hard thing,' says the writer, 'to present the conditions and tendencies, which it is the purpose of this enquiry to elicit, within the framework of a questionnaire in which the words "organisation" and "professional" appear so frequently. The life of the Church in Burma approaches more closely to the spontaneity of apostolic times than to the highly organised and professionalised work of the Churches in the West, for better or for worse. In the freshness, simplicity and ardour of the workers, for better; in regard to training and such aids as religious literature that make for the best use of time and effort, for worse. But to estimate correctly the life and work of women in the Church in Burma requires a perceptiveness and elasticity of mind that can recognise life and the possibility of its development along other lines than those indicated by your questions.' Nonetheless, this report does break out of the straight-jacket of the questions and tell its own tale of the work of women, especially of the Biblewomen. They are common to the American and to the English missions working in Burma, and facilities for giving them some sort of training exist in all the three language groups of the country among whom mission work is described, that is the Burmans, the Kachins and the Karens. Some of these women are teachers, some are nurses and the variety of the work they do is an indication only of the opportunities that are available. The American Baptist is much the largest mission in Burma, and its work ranges from the simplest evangelism in the villages to the magnificent Judson College. Biblewomen are trained in each of the three languages. The social customs of the different groups vary. The Burmans treat their women with great reserve and dislike co-education, while the Karens are used to it from the village school on, as are also the Kachin hill people. So when a Bible school was opened for Kachin men, six women presented themselves on the opening day. When told that there was not even any place for them to sleep they replied that they could easily build themselves a grass hut in the compound, and so began their training with the men. 'The course is three years and most of the girls take the entire course.' Their numbers are increasing. The largest number of women in training are the Karens, for they are the largest group within the Church. The people are keenly evangelistic and strong supporters of their schools, scattered about the villages. Most of the girls coming to be trained are country girls, with a low standard of education. Their villages supply them with no chances of work except to plant rice in the fields, and they look to the Church for something different to do. The standard of education 'is steadily being raised and the trend will be towards a more highly educated body of women, though not relatively so, for the general standard of education is rising'. Some of these women are employed by the women's societies in the Karen Church to act as missionaries in the remote villages, some are nurses, some go where there are no pastors, for ordination is sparingly given among the Karens and many a man works for years as a pastor without receiving ordination. The Bible-woman turns her hand to everything, including all the ministry of the Church in some places, except the administration of the Sacraments.

It would be possible to quote from other reports. There are certainly places where the Biblewoman is still of the old sort: her usefulness is growing less as the general standard of education rises and as the greater freedom of women in non-Christian com-munities permit of more varied activities among women than house to house visitation. Wherever progress is being made it is on the lines of more selective recruitment and better training, so that the difference between the new style Biblewoman of the East, no longer called by that name, and the woman parish worker of the West will tend to disappear.

The report from Burma has an account of a unique relationship of Christian women teachers to the work of the Church. It is worth quoting as a whole.

'A paragraph must be given to the *Sayamas* of the Christian schools of Burma. "Saya" means teacher, still a term of honour, affection and respect in this country, and "ma" is the feminine affix.

'The mission schools and their teachers hold a place of intimate and vital relation to the Church that has no counterpart in America, unless it is in the parish schools of the Roman Church. They form usually so large a proportion of the educated members of a community that they are found to be the backbone of the local church and the spear-head of its activity. This is not true alone of mission schools. In Loikaw, one of the Administered States, the staff of the State school is entirely Christian, and since the destruction of the local church during the war, the Sunday services have been held in the school building. This is one of the cases in which the Church would be a missionary Church and its members missionaries as well as teachers. A large proportion of these teachers are women. That they consider theirs a religious calling as well as a secular profession has been abundantly shown since the war.

'The new Government of Burma proposes no longer to give grants in aid to mission schools, but to establish at least one government free school in each locality. Since the mission schools in general have had a high reputation the Government has in a number of cases offered this position to the mission school. This offer might be considered a most advantageous and enviable one, since it would mean for the teachers of the school good salaries and an assured future, with pensions on retirement, but these offers have been declined because it would mean giving up religious teaching in the school, and its distinctively Christian character. They have preferred the meagre salary that can be afforded from the small fees paid by the children and a completely uncertain future. It is not the Mission that has made this decision. Before the missionaries had returned to Burma or the Japanese had left its borders the Sayamas were re-opening the schools, gathering in the children by the hundreds, often to shell-damaged and battered buildings, with few books and almost no equipment, carrying on on their own initiative and responsibility, forming school boards from among good friends in the community.

'In Moulmein there were before the war two of the largest Baptist Mission schools in the country, the Morton Lane Girls' High School and the Judson Boys' High School. Sayama Daw Nyein Tha has re-organised these two and she and her teachers are carrying them on as a co-educational school in what buildings are left of the Morton Lane School. Sayama Daw Hla Shein has done the same for the Kemmendine Girls' school in Rangoon, first in a rented building and now in the few remaining buildings on the school compound. This has been possible because of the reputation of these schools; both Christian and Buddhist parents prefer, if they can afford it, to pay to send their children to these Christian schools, rather than to the Government free school.

'Sayama Daw Thein, of Henzada, was the first Burmese woman to be put in charge of one of the A.B.M. Burmese Girls' Schools. She managed, with courage, wisdom and untiring devotion to keep her school going throughout almost the entire period of the war, winning the respect of the Japanese invaders, and being turned out of the school buildings only once, by a company of the Burma Independence Army. When the income from fees was not enough to pay the teachers she started a coffee business to help support the school. Through all difficulties and dangers she kept the school on an even keel, an oasis of order and discipline during the chaotic conditions of war.

'There is no field of service where Christians in Burma have shown more initiative, devotion, willingness to sacrifice, hard work and sound sense than these women teachers in the mission schools, nor one that has made a greater contribution to the Christian Church in that place.

'Two Burmese Sayamas of the Anglican Church were offered the choice of recanting their faith or being beheaded, and chose death, and among the martyrs of the Karen Church there were women, and children as well, who went to their death singing. Though this falls under no category of Christian service, martyrdom has profoundly to do with the health and vitality of the Church, and its power to propagate its faith.'

RELIGIOUS ORDERS AND COMMUNITIES OF WOMEN

The first chapter of this book referred to the disappearance from all Protestant Churches at the Reformation, of religious orders for men and for women. In the mixture of feelings upon which the Reformation was carried along, anti-monasticism was an extremely strong element. There was a revolt of sentiment not only against the abuse of the monasteries, their wealth and power, but against the whole idea of a renunciation of the world. One of the popular outcries of the time against the monks was, why could they not marry and shoulder their burdens in the world like other men? With the monasteries went the nunneries, and with them the only means by which women could practice a complete withdrawal from the world, or a corporate Christian life of disciplined prayer and service. It made no difference in the years that followed the Reformation that the convents and nunneries had been decadent, they were not wanted even in a purified form.

In the Lutheran and the Reformed Churches in all parts of the world, religious orders and communities have never been generally restored, though there have been isolated groups of women who have lived a life approximating to that of nuns. In the Anglican Church they were restored a hundred years ago, and in the Orthodox Churches they have survived in emasculated form and attempts have been made in different countries within the Orthodox Churches to revive them in a modern form. In the Syrian Orthodox Church of South India the Ashram is an Indian form of a religious community. There are also various attempts in other Churches to revive some of the features of religious orders.

The revival of religious orders[1] in the Anglican Church was a part of the nineteenth century movement to recover the lost heritage of Catholicism for the Anglican Church. This was a liturgical and doctrinal movement, and the religious orders of men and women grew out of that movement as an expression of the desire to recover the full Catholic tradition of worship. The main purpose in withdrawing from the world was not to do good works but to offer prayer and worship under discipline: the good works came as the expression of worship in life. There are over fifty Anglican religious orders and communities in England, some are entirely contemplative, some are active and some are mixed. They vary in size from the small community under one roof carrying out a single piece of work such as a convalescent home or an orphanage, with as few as a dozen members, to the largest orders with several hundred members working in the mother house or in branches at home or overseas. St. Mary's Convent, Wantage, is one of the oldest and the largest, founded in 1848: the convent now governs thirty branch houses in England, India and South Africa.

Women who wish to enter a religious order must be members of the Church of England, or in some cases of a Church in communion with it. The usual practice is to accept a woman as a postulant for several months, so that she can live in the house and observe the life by taking part in it. At the end of these months, if she wishes to continue and the authorities are prepared to accept her, she is clothed as a novice and is appointed her tasks in the Community. The length of the Novitiate varies in the different Communities, an average length being two or three years. At the end of this period the Novice, if elected by the Chapter of the Community, proceeds to Profession, taking the three Vows of Poverty, Chastity and Obedience. In an increasing number of Communities these Vows are in the first instance taken for a short period not exceeding six years; they may be taken for a stated period of three or five years or renewed annually. These Vows are called Simple or Temporary Vows. The members of most Communities take life vows, whether at the end of the Novitiate or

[1] The language used to describe the organisation of religious communities is ancient and full of technicalities. Of the many religious communities within the Anglican church only a very small number can properly be referred to as 'orders'.

after this preliminary period, and these are received by the Bishop who may in some cases be the Visitor of the Community. The Superior of a Community is elected by the Chapter, consisting of all the professed sisters, although in some Communities, especially if the houses are scattered about the world, each house is independent to the extent of electing its own Superior and its own novices and professed sisters. Spiritual authority is shared by the Superior with the Warden or the Chaplain General of the Community who administer the Rule under which the sisters live. Most of these Rules are based on the Rule of St. Benedict or, less frequently, on that of St. Augustine. Some are entirely modern. In the case of communities which have much foreign missionary work, rules are devised to suit such conditions. The Rule normally prescribes the hours to be given to prayer, the regulation of the interior life of the sisters, and their relations to each other and to the outside world. The vow of poverty demands that professed sisters shall give up control of their private means to the community, and the rule of obedience means that a sister must serve in any place or at any form of work decided on by the Superior. There is always a chaplain attached to each house within an order who administers the Sacraments and hears confession.

The vocation to the life of a Religious is a personal call from God to a life of prayer: the period of the novitiate is a testing of that call. It is open to the novice to withdraw at any time and it is a part of the spiritual duty of the Superior to help the novice to see whether or not she has a vocation to the life. Election by the Chapter is the ratification of the inner call of the individual by the community as a whole: it does not in itself constitute the call, which is of God to the individual soul.

The practical work of the different orders and communities tends of necessity towards specialisation. Some are mainly teaching orders, the sisters serving on the staff of schools controlled by the order: others are mainly concerned with hospitals, usually small ones for special types of cases, especially those for which the nursing is distasteful, or convalescent homes and homes for old people. Many communities run orphanages, a few specialise in moral welfare work, others do general parish work, visiting the homes, and one also trains lay parish workers. The sisters for the most part do their own domestic work and sometimes gardening

also. A number of communities have a retreat house attached to
their premises where they receive guests who come either for a
time of personal withdrawal from the world in prayer, or for
organised retreats. The influence of this work on the parish life
and on many organisations in the Church of England has been
very great during the past half century, as the habit of making
retreats has grown. A great variety exists in the overseas work of
the orders, some of which accept sisters from among the people
with whom they work (thus one has a Korean sisterhood), while
others train African and Indian women for work in schools,
hospitals and homes.

The Canadian report mentions the Order of the Sisters of St.
John the Divine, whose work includes schools, hospitals and
homes. It also mentions the sisters of an English community
working in several parts of Canada, the Community of the Sisters
of the Church. The Australian report mentions the existence of
Anglican communities in that country. There are two Anglican
communities in New Zealand, one in Auckland and the other in
Christchurch. In South Africa six are mentioned, four of which
are branches of English mother houses. One is an African Community. Most of the work of these communities is among Africans
or coloured people.

There are thirteen religious communities for women in the
Protestant Episcopal Church of America. They are recognised in
the Canon Law of the Church and certain regulations are there
prescribed for them. One of the Orders is contemplative, four are
active and eight are mixed. The work covers the same range as
in Great Britain.

Religious Communities are also to be found in the Scottish
Episcopal Church: five are mentioned in the report. Some are
indigenous to Scotland while others are Scottish branches of
English Communities.

In the Orthodox Church of Greece there are also traces to be
seen today of a long tradition of the monastic life. The word
'traces' is used advisedly, for there was a time when monasteries
and nunneries and mixed houses were thick on the ground and
some of them were of great size and power. Many remain, most
of them in isolated places cut off from the world, small in size. A
survey of the nunneries of Greece was made in 1919 by Professor
Alivizatos of the University of Athens, and since then no further

survey has been made. His report makes gloomy reading. Some
of the nunneries had as few as three nuns, many of the nuns in
others were illiterate. Among the larger nunneries there was a
higher proportion of better educated women, some even conducting small schools. Handwork, weaving, the cultivation of
gardens and olive orchards, cheesemaking and other pursuits,
some of them involving heavy manual labour, occupy the nuns'
time and make their livelihood. Some of the nunneries were once
monasteries. There is one modern order of nuns, the Order of
the Apostle Peter, founded by the Archimandrite Peter Vlotildiz.
This nunnery of St. Ierotheos at Megara is a remarkable place.
The women were recruited from among the educated classes and
were trained for their work by the founder, who paid careful
attention to the needs of each particular group of nuns—two of
them, for example, have read for degrees in Political Science.
There was no organisation whatever in which such women as
these nuns could be employed in the Church, and their services
were therefore offered to the State and used in three ways. The
Department of Justice accepted their service at the Central Prisons
for women, where they soon were holding positions of responsibility which they filled to the satisfaction of all concerned,
including fellow employees. The nuns were present and were
wounded when the prison was attacked and bombarded during
the war. Another group of nuns was appointed to the State
Reformatory, and a third to a Children's Home, also a State
institution. One of them became Director of this last institution.

The women's branch of the Zöe movement has some of the
features of a religious order, though it could also be described as
a movement of highly educated women working for evangelism
through the Church. In order that the reader unacquainted with
the background of Orthodox Church life in Greece may understand this movement a few general remarks are necessary. In the
Greek Orthodox Church there are more laymen than priests with
degrees in theology. Priests are mainly concerned with the reading
of the liturgical services and the administration of the Sacraments.
Many of them are ordained in later life and have no theological or
any other academic qualifications. They work closely under their
bishops. Everything in the Church is organised under the bishops
and there are seventy-four dioceses, some of them not much
bigger than a large parish. The bishop is frequently assisted by

priest-monks who live with him and form his staff. Since the priests are not a particularly well-educated class they sometimes do not preach at all, and there are often sermons either in church or in a lecture room delivered at a different time from the regular service by a layman, or even in some cases by a woman. It is also a custom to have 'catechetical schools' for the teaching of church doctrine. The Zöe ('life') movement started some forty-five years ago. It is a brotherhood of men, all theologically trained, who are celibates and have a community house. About a third of them are priests, the rest are lay theologians. They wear lay dress and are a free movement, not directly controlled by the Church, but wholly given to its work. They travel and organise catechetical schools, they write and have a publishing house, and they have fathered movements of the laity under their spiritual guidance. They have all the devotion of monks and are really in most respects a religious order. The female counterpart of this movement is Eusebia (Piety) (presumably named after the Archimandrite Eusebius Mattho-poulos, the founder of Zöe). It was organised in 1938. It is a closed society and the number of members is small. All are uni-versity graduates and the aim is primarily missionary. It works all over Greece, fostering local movements, especially among the more educated and younger women of Greece. Eusebia is the movement in Greece which looks after the Sunday Schools, pro-duces literature and trains teachers. Older girls are enlisted to visit in hospitals, and from the ex-scholars of the Sunday Schools Eusebia has formed groups of young workers. The work of the Student Christian Movement among women is largely run by members of Eusebia. The movement also works among nurses and forms the counterpart of a nurses' Christian fellowship in other countries. It has a rest home for nurses in Athens. It pene-trates the State schools and universities and some of its members teach on the staffs of these institutions. The missionary journeys of Eusebia have quite an apostolic ring about them, as one reads the lists of provincial towns and islands visited by the members who organise meetings and catechetical schools for country-women. There is no real counterpart of this organisation in any other country.

In Russia a remarkable attempt was made in the late nineteenth century by a single woman of very great vision to revive the religious life among women. She was the Countess Eugenia

Efimovsky, a woman of distinguished family and education. The loss of the family's fortunes, and a fire which left her a cripple, reduced her to earning her living by writing, but she was really a woman of immense vigour. At thirty-five she made her profession as a nun and was sent to Lesna, in a western province of Russia, to do missionary work. Her ideal was monastic life with practical Christian service, and she succeeded in creating one of the greatest teaching establishments in Russia with a thousand orphan girls under her care. The place was a genuine cultural centre for the life of a whole region. She thought that the actual state of convents in Russia was very low, and she wanted to revive the ancient order of deaconesses. She wrote some powerful pamphlets on this subject, but she could not move the Holy Synod, even with the support of the Royal Family. She was caught between the immovability of the old Church and the swift rise of the Russian revolution. Her convent had to leave Russia and she died in Serbia.

Her spiritual successor was a woman born in like circumstances and similarly dogged by tragedy, Elizabeth Skobtzoff. She was a poet and writer, and a friend of some of the leading Russian writers. She had a passion for social justice, was a revolutionary but fell foul of Bolshevik methods. She was imprisoned and later went to Paris, losing both her daughters. Here she set to work to keep alive among an emigré people the culture of their faith. An old garage became a church and she painted the ikons, and travelled about giving lectures both to working groups in the suburbs, and to students through the Russian Student Christian Movement. At the same time she was organising a great social work, which she called 'monasticism in the world', first a hostel for young Russian girls and then a home for old people, all under her own care. The unemployed, the destitute and the utterly unloved found help and understanding in her; she was known to the drunks and the syphilitic wrecks of humanity who haunted the banks of the Seine as she trudged to the market in her well-known men's boots, fetching food which she got cheap from the merchants and serving it in the canteens for the unemployed, and she visited in the slums. During the German occupation she opened her house to Jews and she perished in the gas chambers of the concentration camp of Ravensbruck in 1943, while her son and the priest of her parish who had helped her in her work both met their deaths in similar fashion at Buchenwald. Soon she was a legend among those who had known her in the camp and her work continued in Paris. Two of her helpers founded another community near Melun, and from this yet another small community grew, devoted to the care of sick children.

It is not easy to convey the spirit of the Russian Orthodox Church in Paris by cutting up the witness of so small a community into sub-sections. There is scarcely a member of it who has not suffered in some way or another, and those who were not emigrés of the revolutionary period have come from Estonia and the other Baltic States through the Displaced Persons' camps within the last few years. Poverty is the main mark of this Church, and mutual service arises from it, so that it is scarcely right to name the nuns as though their service were peculiarly withdrawn. The whole community is, in a sense, a withdrawal from the world, from all the world they knew, and the nun is not an unknown anonymous person away in a convent, but visible in the life of the parish and known to all—as indeed many nuns elsewhere are too.

The report from Egypt mentions the existence of religious orders for women in the Coptic Church, though details are not given. In India a close indigenous parallel to the monastic order is the Ashram in its true Indian sense, and not in the popular use of it as a temporary retreat. There are many ashrams for men in India and Ceylon, Hindu and Christian. In Travancore the Bethel Ashram was started thirty years ago. There are now fourteen permanent and fifteen other women workers trained for work in the villages. Normally they are sent in pairs, and work in a single area for three years, closely associated with the pastor. As well as the mother house behind them, the sisters have the support of the prayers and voluntary service of the two hundred members of the Ashram Fellowship.

In Lebanon the Kalfayan Religious Order was founded in 1865 by a woman of the Armenian Church, Serpouhi Kalfayan, who watched the foundation of religious orders of the Roman Catholic Church in the near East, and knew herself to have a vocation for the religious life. In an epidemic of cholera she started a small orphanage for the children of victims. A year later the institution and the sisters whom she had gathered to run it were recognised by the Patriarch of Jerusalem. Help in financing a building came from the Sultan Aziz and from many supporters. The work has

continued and the sisters of the order are ordained as deaconesses
by the Patriarch of Jerusalem.

It will be seen from the foregoing that the Religious Orders
in which women make solemn and lifelong vows, and bind themselves to live together in communities under discipline, only exist
in the Orthodox Churches, where they belong to a very ancient
tradition, and in the Anglican Church where they have been
revived in the last 100 years as part of the Catholic revival
within that Church. Some Anglican orders have '3rd orders'—
tertiaries or lay members, who live under a Rule adapted to living
in the world. A part of the Rule consists in making a specified
number of retreats in the year. There are in many other Churches
distinct signs of groups of people who are feeling after one or
another feature of the Religious Orders and Communities. The
liturgical society in the Dutch Reformed Church considered before
the war the possibility of becoming a religious order with a
discipline, but the idea was abandoned. It holds conferences on
liturgical subjects and wishes also to hold retreats. At least two
ministers in the Dutch Reformed Church hold retreats of some
twenty to thirty people in their parsonages. One has, with his
wife, given up parish work in order to concentrate more fully on
the work of retreats and of giving personal guidance. A Dutch
Baptist minister has also worked out a form of retreat, and held a
considerable number both for specialised groups of social workers,
teachers, etc. and for general groups. The same development is
noted also in France. Other movements seek not so much the
element of withdrawal as that of fellowship in work and a simple
discipline. This is to be found in the French Cimade, the small
teams of young people in this work living together in a simple
Rule. In some cases the church authorities have allowed particular
leaders of these groups to celebrate the sacrament of Holy Communion. The French report also gives an account of a fellowship
in Madagascar—a kind of religious order called the Society of the
Disciples of the Lord. It was founded by a Malagasy and consists
of men and women. They have a community house from which
they go out to villages in twos, preaching and healing by the
laying on of hands. They work in accord with the churches. A
religious community of women at Grandchamp Neuchatel runs
a retreat house and lives a communal religious life under discipline.
Its members belong to the Swiss Reformed Church. Several

fellowships of women with a rule of life have been started in Germany since the war. If all the facts could be known of these small groups in different countries, who are trying under the pressure of modern life to master the ceaseless rush of events, and to make time for prayer and introduce some discipline into their daily lives, they would certainly show that the hunger in the lives of Christians for some of the virtues recovered for the Church in the Religious Orders cannot possibly be measured simply in terms of the number of women who take the veil.

THE WOMAN WITH HIGH THEOLOGICAL QUALIFICATIONS

It is important for the purpose of this study to distinguish between two types of theological training given to women. On the one hand there is the kind of training which has been worked out to suit different classes of women workers for the Church— missionary training, training for church workers, deaconesses, church sisters, etc. This is vocational training, suited to the work the woman is to do, with a theological content based mainly on the study of the Bible in the language of the student. On the other hand there is the full theological course, including the study of Greek and perhaps of Hebrew, leading to a university honours degree or its equivalent. In some countries, when a woman has completed this course successfully she has every qualification for the full ordained ministry of the Church, and the only barrier is her sex: in other countries she has all the academic qualifications needed short of being admitted for the final training of the ordination candidate in pastoralia, or allowed to sit for the final examination. The woman who enters upon the first type of training knows that there is a job for her at the end of it and what, within reasonable certainty, that job will be. Probably she is financially helped by her Church, or the organisation she will serve, to meet the cost of the training. The woman who undertakes the full theological course does so almost always at her own risk and charges. There is no guarantee that a Church or organisation will want her services at the end of her training. For the most part, therefore, the women who embark on this long and stiff course of study are strongly drawn to it, most of them do well in consequence and most of them have considerable determination to carry them through a good deal of discouragement on the way.

In Europe (including Great Britain) this higher training in theology is usually obtained at a University. When Universities grew up in the Middle Ages theology was one of the chief subjects of study. It was the 'queen of the sciences', a proper study for all Christian men of culture and not for clerics only. Theological faculties have survived down the ages in most of the older universities of Europe, though few pursue this course whose destination is other than the ordained ministry—except the women. The so-called 'modern universities' founded under secular liberal influences in the nineteenth century do not as a rule contain theological faculties. When the universities were opened to women the theological faculties were also opened at the same time, or shortly after. There therefore exists all over Europe the means whereby a woman can obtain the same academic qualifications as the minister. The Churches, if they wished to do so, would be powerless to prevent them. In England the Church of England has itself provided the equivalent of a university honours degree in theology in the Lambeth Diploma, held by 173 women since its inception in 1906 and recognised by the Ministry of Education as the equivalent of a degree. In the United States and Canada theological education is carried on in Seminaries or Divinity Schools, some of which will admit women (some with a strict limitation of numbers) and some of which will not.

Short of ordination, what do these women do? It should perhaps be made clear that unless a woman is a member of a Church which already ordains women, she does not read theology at the university in the not very well grounded hope that her Church will change its mind before she is qualified (although the Scottish report tells of two women who did this and subsequently became Congregationalists). One thing that is striking is the comparatively large number of women studying theology who belong to Churches which do not and are not likely to ordain women to the full ministry. There are, for example, some two hundred women theological students in Germany, although it is known that the Church is receding from the full ordination of women.

There are two main lines of occupation for these women: they are teachers in schools, training colleges and universities, or they are employed by the Church and by church organisations.

It is not unnatural that in those countries where there is the teaching of theology in universities, there is also religious instruction in schools. In the United States the separation of Church and State, upheld by the American constitution, precludes the teaching of the Christian religion in State schools, and there is therefore no place for women with theological degrees as the employees of State schools or State colleges. In Germany, Austria, Scandinavia, Great Britain, Brazil and some cantons of Switzerland, Christian teaching is required in the State schools. In Great Britain both religious (Christian) instruction, based on one of a number of syllabuses agreed between the denominations, and a daily act of corporate school worship are compulsory by Act of Parliament in all State schools since 1944. A considerable number of women with theological qualifications, therefore, teach in schools. In Europe this is sometimes done on a part-time basis, combined with some church work. In Great Britain it is more customary for the teacher to be a full-timer, although only in a large school will there be enough religious teaching to occupy all her time. In Germany, Austria and Switzerland there are associations of theologically trained women which bring them into contact with each other. There is no such organisation in Britain, though the Institute of Christian Education gives teachers of religion in schools and colleges advice on books, refresher courses and the chance of meeting for discussion in local branches.

In Great Britain a considerable number of women with theological qualifications work in the schools and in training colleges for teachers, both Church colleges and State, where there is great opportunity for them to reach hundreds of young people who do not come to the churches. A number of teachers of other subjects have given their spare time to the study of theology, or have taken leave of absence in order to read for a university degree or diploma in theology, or for the Lambeth diploma. The standard of religious teaching in girls' schools is infinitely better than in boys' because of the pains women have taken to get themselves well qualified. A new experiment is the William Temple College which is providing for lay women from many walks of life a course of study which combines theology with sociology in an attempt to give to students a Christian approach to modern problems of man in society. There are few women in Great Britain with theological degrees who are working in the parishes, though some deaconesses hold the Lambeth Diploma. A larger number are to be found on the staffs or as principals of training institutions for the Church and Christian organisations. Good theological qualifications are being more and more highly valued both by individual women and by the bodies who employ them, not least the missionary societies.

In Germany, Switzerland and Austria more women of this class are to be found in the parishes because there is a distinctive office for them, of which the nearest counterpart in Britain is the deaconess. This is the Vikarin (woman curate or assistant to the minister). They have the same training as ministers, but in general they are not ordained, but *eingesegnet*, dedicated. Both the dedication and the duties of the Vikarinnen vary from one regional Church to another. 'In some Churches, e.g. Hanover' says the German report, 'this dedication is hardly distinguishable in form and content from the ordination of a minister. But there is a difference in the authority given to each'. In some provincial Churches the Vikarin is not allowed to do more than the parish worker, i.e. to work among women and children and to teach and preach only to them. Baden and Schleswig Holstein make it possible for an individual Vikarin to receive a licence from the church authorities to hold a parochial service and to administer the Sacraments. The Old Prussian Church allows women to hold services and administer the Sacraments in women's hospitals, prisons and institutions. In addition, in special circumstances permission is given to preach and administer the Sacraments in the parishes. Another regulation of this Church is that each Vikarin must be given an independent sphere of activity of her own. In actual facts fewer women are in these posts than the existence of the regulations might be taken to indicate, many of them being wholly occupied in teaching. The total number of 'dedicated' Vikarinnen is about 250, including those in schools, parish work and special posts in the Inner Mission and in institutions of all kinds. In the East where pastors are very few in proportion to the work, Vikarinnen are in greater and greater demand and are steadily being given greater responsibilities.

During the war and the confusion which followed the defeat many of the Vikarinnen performed the duties of pastors in exceedingly difficult situations. This work is not described here because it belongs more appropriately in the chapter on the ordination of women.

In the German report one of the Vikarinnen, who is working in a women's maternity hospital, describes the opportunities which come to her in her work. Women whose normal lives allow no time for recollection find themselves with time to spare and the experience of being looked after instead of ceaselessly caring for others. These are the normally healthy who are happy in the birth of their children. But there are many others, those who lose their child, those who have the eighth or ninth and wonder how another mouth is to be fed. Above all, there is the woman whose child is not her husband's, or the unmarried woman who has, while she is lying in bed, to take the responsibility for the child she has so much resented or even hated before birth. There is the woman who has done herself grave injury by attempted abortion, or who is diseased. The Vikarin who makes this large public hospital her sole field of service comes to know all the signs, to understand the deceptions which cover a wounded spirit, and she is greatly strengthened in the work by the fact that she can administer baptism in the hospital. Nearly all these women are uprooted from the parish: even the formal connection has been broken: but 'with five to eight children to baptise, one can reckon on a congregation of twenty-five to thirty visitors, mostly men. The address at the baptism, the impressive Lutheran liturgy offer a unique opportunity to speak to the parents about the miracle of creation and their Christian responsibilities. . . . It is possible to speak in more detail beforehand to the mother and afterwards to the father. It is remarkable how the fathers at first come to discharge what seems to them a necessary civic act, but when it is over they are in a different and more thoughtful frame of mind. Many fathers attach great importance to it and insist on holding the baby themselves over the font. On high Festival days a baptism is celebrated with all the staff and patients as congregation. The nurses make preparation for the baptism and in this way are drawn into an active part in this Christian act'.

In Switzerland all six universities grant degrees in theology and make no difference in the acceptance of men and women students. Since all religious affairs are in the hands of the cantons, different regulations prevail for the acceptance of women for work in the churches, and there are five different examinations for the women theologians. 'The most usual arrangement is for a woman to work with the name of *Assistant Minister* beside one or more ministers in a congregation.' However, where congregations are widely scattered a woman may have *de facto* charge of a branch congregation. As Assistant Minister the woman's duties may vary from sharing in all the work of the parish to being given one part of the work, such as youth work, hospital visiting or the charitable work of the parish. 'By now,' says the report, 'the congregations and, above all, individual church members in different places have learned to appreciate the service of a woman theologian. But yet, whenever there is anywhere a new post to be created or an existing one to be filled, the old doubts and objections are expressed.'

In the Dutch Reformed Church there are twenty-five women who are pastors' assistants and have university theological qualifications. They have taken a four-year theological course, but are not allowed to sit the third examination which gives entry to the ministry. In 1945 twenty women students enrolled for the theological course in Leyden University. In 1944 an advertisement put in a church newspaper produced twenty letters from parishes wanting pastors' assistants: but the terms on which the parishes want these are not very happy. The pay is extremely poor, and usually they are not allowed to attend the meetings of the church trustees or of pastors, so that they work very much in the dark and on their own. The Church is trying to put pressure on trustees to give these workers a proper wage and to arrange for pensions. The women who can work in such financial conditions are usually from the upper middle classes. The report remarks that congregations definitely prefer women with theological degrees to lower qualified workers.

The report from Finland says that there are about fifty women with university qualifications in theology. Most of them are absorbed in teaching, but some are in parish work, doing the same things as have been described elsewhere, and there is, says the report, a great demand for more of these women ministers' assistants, (who are not ordained) because of the acute shortage of ministers.

In Austria the first women took their theological degrees nearly thirty years ago, and immediately before the war ten per cent. of theological students were women. The numbers fell sharply during the war and have not recovered. Until the Nazis forbade Christian teaching in the schools, most of these women were teachers, but after 1938 they began to work in the parishes, and some went to Germany where there were more opportunities at

I

the time. The training is exactly the same as that of a minister, eight half-yearly periods of study at a university for the *pro candidature* examinations are followed by two years as an assistant to a minister before the *pro ministerio* examination. She is not allowed to preach or to administer the Sacraments, though a later decree allows her to preach in emergency. After a trial of two years she is installed as a Vikarin. The main work of the Vikarinnen in Austria has been as assistants to ministers in the city churches and as travelling pastors among the scattered village congregation, in the north of the country.

In Hungary women also may sit for the same theological examinations as men candidates for the ministry. The theological course lasts for five years and is followed by a year of practical work after which they may sit for the minister's examination. Women are admitted to church theological colleges, but the church law prescribes that when they have passed the ministerial examination 'Women in possession of a minister's qualifications may be employed only as teachers, professors of religion in elementary schools and in deaconess service; they may not undertake preaching or liturgical work.'

Chaplains' Assistants. A great opportunity opened up during the war for women with theological qualifications or with pastoral experience. When women were conscripted into the Army, Navy and Air Force in Great Britain, a representative committee of church women of five denominations approached the War Office in 1940, and succeeded in convincing the Secretary of State for War that the pastoral care of the very large number of women drafted into the women's forces could not be properly carried out by men chaplains alone. The recruitment and supervision of the assistants remained in the hands of the Committee for Churches' Work for Women in the Forces, and they were assigned to places at home and abroad where there were numbers of women in two of the three services, the Army and the Air Force. In a very few cases the women found that the chaplains somewhat resented their appointment and did not give them much to do, but this was exceptional. In almost all cases the arrangement was soon working well, and the assistants were conducting Bible classes, Confirmation classes or preparation classes for church member-ship, conducting informal services and doing a great deal of

pastoral work with individuals. The arrangement has been continued since the war. In addition to the chaplains' assistants (of
whom at the peak there were thirty), the Churches' Committee
raised the money to pay for thirty-four district organisers who
arranged for the help of three hundred volunteers who helped in
a variety of ways from lecturing to hospital visiting. The attitude
of the forces constituted 'an unprecedented acknowledgment by
the State of the importance of women's church work'. After the
war the Royal Air Force took a further step by appointing an
ordained woman (Congregationalist) to work among women in
that service.

In Australia and in New Zealand inter-denominational groups
of women tried to obtain the same facilities for women to work
among women in the forces, but failed, largely because the
numbers were not thought by the authorities to justify it.

In Canada a similar approach was made and was successful.
Five women were appointed—two Anglican, one Presbyterian,
one Baptist and one United Church of Canada: all were trained
church workers and in addition took the same training as officers
in the Canadian Women's Army Corps. Their duties were those
just described. 'It is impossible to estimate the lasting value of this
service in bringing the Church and its work to the thoughtful
attention of those young women who had responded to the call of
their country. Many were led into full membership with the
Church and some have entered its full-time service.' (Canadian
report).

Switzerland, though it was not at war maintained a state of
preparedness against attack throughout the war, with large numbers of men under arms. Here women found another means of
contriving somewhat the same end. They got themselves accepted
on a voluntary basis as assistants to the chaplains, some of them
to do welfare work and others, with the training, to do pastoral
work, especially in the military hospitals with their very large
numbers of women staff. They were appointed by the military
authorities, through the Red Cross doctors.

The answers of all other countries on this question were
negative, the opportunities not having been given for work of
this kind. Much voluntary work with the forces was done by
women in very many countries, mostly in the nature of canteens,
clubs, hospitality and hospital visiting.

WOMEN AND THE ORDAINED MINISTRY

D URING the past thirty years there has been debate in many Churches about the ordination of women. The debate has not been universal (there are Churches in which the matter has never been discussed, including all the Churches of the Orthodox communion), nor has it been continuous. It may arise over some particular point involving deeper issues of principle, and then die down again. The form of the debate varies very much: in some Churches it goes on only among small groups of interested men and women who have no official standing in the Church in relation to the matter. Groups form round some active person who perhaps writes a book on the subject: here and there groups within a Church shape a policy and work to get it accepted by the Church as a whole. The subject of the ordination of women occasionally brings together inter-denominational groups, for there are always those in Churches which do not ordain women who want to know more about the Churches in which the ministry of women is accepted. Some Churches have had the matter debated and put to the vote in their highest courts, and have appointed official commissions to study the matter and report to the whole Church.

Why is the matter ever discussed at all, seeing that for centuries the very idea of ordaining women to the ministry was unthought of and unthinkable? The answer to that question is that although the reasons why the matter has come up for debate at a particular moment vary from Church to Church, there is only one main reason why a matter undiscussed for nineteen centuries is now a subject of serious study and lively debate, that is the radical change in the place of women in society in the last fifty years. The Churches have themselves helped to bring about that change, especially by their significant contribution to the education of women. Women can and do complete successfully long courses of study, discharge responsible posts in the professions, in social service, in politics (especially in local government) and in business. These facts, even if they refer only to a minority of women, raise the question, what about the Church?

But the question is raised in many different forms. 'Why should the Christian ministry be the only or almost the only profession barred to women on the grounds of their sex?' This form of the question, it should be said at the outset of this chapter, is not the form in which it is heard in the Church itself, it is not even the question asked by the most ardent Christian supporters of the cause of the ordination of women. This is society's form of the question, and it will be heard in groups working for women's rights, among whom Christians will no doubt be found, and to which, in that context, some may subscribe. Even the most ardent supporters of the ordination of women do not usually fall head-long into the error of equating *simpliciter* the Christian ministry with 'the professions' or of urging the Church to take a certain course of action for the purpose of bringing itself into line with society and clearing itself of the charge of obscurantism. The form in which the question is asked within many Churches is much more nearly this: 'the Church needs all the service that can be given: the work it is called on to do is far beyond the strength of its appointed leaders, who are the clergy. It is not only in need of willing help but of trained help. Women exist who are both willing and trained. How is the Church to make use of their services?' The answering of this question by any Church involves the examination of many possible answers. In some Churches—the Roman Catholic and the Orthodox Churches are the chief examples—the work of lay women may be vigorously discussed, usually in reference to some practical need, without the question of women in the priesthood being even mentioned. The very idea just does not occur. There is scope for women in the social work of the Churches and in education, and if their calling is to prayer there are convents. The prevailing view of the ministry in both the Roman Catholic and the Orthodox Churches is strongly sacerdotal. They also lay strong emphasis on the tradition and history of the Church. 'The place of women in the Church in Orthodox theology has always been considered as a helping and not an executive one' (Russian Orthodox in Paris). 'The work and place of women in the Church were defined long ago, from the beginning, and once settled, the question does not arise again', (Coptic Catholic Church in Egypt). But it is important not to identify the Orthodox with the Roman Catholic attitude to the service of women in the Church, for the Eastern Orthodox Church preserved for many centuries an order of deaconesses who were ordained by their bishops and assisted at the Holy Com- munion: a form of ordination of women, although not practised in the modern Orthodox Churches, is therefore a part of their tradition. In the Roman Church (west) deaconesses do not seem to have been ordained by the laying on of hands and were not distinct, as far as can be seen, either from 'widows' on the one hand or from certain consecrated nuns on the other. It has also already been pointed out that a large part of the writing and the teaching of theology in Orthodox Churches is in the hands of the lay theologians. Women share in this work. In Greece they may read theology at the University of Athens. In Paris the Russian Orthodox Church provides a theological training for women.

Many other reports state that the ordained ministry of women is not a matter which is ever discussed. Most of these come from the countries where the prevailing view of women is that they should not exercise leadership of any kind, and are subject to men in all matters. 'The common attitude is strongly against women serving with men. It is based largely on the prevailing attitude towards women in an Oriental and Islamic country. Women should not only not be seen, but not heard either' (Egypt). The report from India notes not only that no Indian women are ordained even in those Churches which ordain women to the ministry in the West, but that ordained women from the West working in India do not usually exercise the functions of the ministry. In Burma a woman who took the full theological course at Judson College, Rangoon, applied for admission to the ministry in the Church founded by the American Baptist Mission, but was refused. Thus social custom may make it impossible for the question of women's ordination to be raised although there is no theological barrier. The report from Hungary says, 'the Hungarian nation comes from an eastern race and has preserved many of its race characteristics to the present day. Women are honoured as wives and mothers but are not regarded as suitable for leadership. Our people however are beginning to adapt themselves to modern times and a woman may adopt any profession except that of minister, for the Church adheres to the opinion of the Bible and the convictions and opinions of the Hungarian people'. This is the only Church of the Reformed tradition in Europe in which the question of women and the ministry has not been discussed, and the reason would appear to be social rather than theological.

A further distinguishable group of Churches are those which have discussed the ordination of women and have opened the full ministry to them on equal terms with men. Of these the Congregational Churches and the Disciples of Christ seem to be the most consistent and universal upholders of the ministry of women. No report of all those received shows a Congregational Church which will not in principle accept women in the ministry on equal terms with men, though in places (New Zealand, for example) no women have been ordained. The Disciples of Christ admit women to the ministry equally with men: 283 women are ministers of this Church in the United States, but only 39 hold pastorates.

The Baptist Church of Great Britain ordains women to the ministry. In the United States (where Baptists are one of the largest confessional groups) the American Baptist Convention (formerly the Northern Baptist Convention) ordains women to the ministry, while the Southern Baptist Convention and the National Baptist Convention of U.S.A. Inc. do not. Smaller Baptist bodies in the United States are divided. In Holland the Mennonites ordain women to the ministry, but only one of the nine Mennonite bodies which figure in the United States report ordains women. Elsewhere (especially in Eastern Europe and Scandinavia, where there are large numbers of Baptists) women are not ordained. 'It is not so much that it is literally impossible as that it is unimaginable' says the report of the Swedish Baptists.

Why has this group of Churches accepted the principle of the equal ministry of men and women? The reason would seem to be in part that their conception of the ministry is less sacerdotal. Wherever the tradition of minister as priest, offering to God the re-presented sacrifice of Christ on behalf of the people is strong, man (i.e. the male) is regarded as the prototype of mankind. But where, as in these Churches, the minister is regarded not solely or even chiefly as priest and as representative in a priestly fashion, but as pastor, preacher and prophet, set aside for a special function from among believers who are all in some sense priests, the idea of a woman minister presents fewer difficulties of that particular kind. But other factors enter into the question. It is clear from the discussion of the ministry of women in many Churches, that a strong argument against it is the fear that a local congregation might find itself with a woman minister against its will. Congregations of the Congregational and Baptist Churches have a high degree of local independence. They may perhaps decide that a woman is all they can afford, but they are unlikely to find a woman —or indeed anybody else—put upon them by authority. Nor do the central bodies of these Churches, when they allow a woman into a theological college, incur any responsibility for finding her a church. If no call to the ministry of a local congregation is made to the woman who seeks a pastorate, the central authorities are not to blame. In fact, they frequently warn women students of the difficulty of finding a church. The American report remarks that although the number of women in the Congregational ministry increases (233 in 1949) 'few of these (84) are in the pastorate it seems.' The Church of the Brethren licenses 'sisters' to preach.

This matter of the autonomy and free choice of the local congregation is one factor in the deliberations of the Methodist Church. The majority against admitting women to the ministry is usually a small one, and that there is no absolute principle in the matter is shown by the willingness of Methodist Churches in the United States, Great Britain and other countries to license women to administer the Sacraments and undertake pastoral duties. In Great Britain the Methodist Conference has explored the matter for some years, rejecting it by a narrowing majority. One argument against the ministry of women is the 'itinerant ministry' characteristic of Methodism. With rare exceptions in Great Britain all Methodist ministers are sent by Conference to a Circuit (a group of congregations under a Superintendent) for a period of three years, sometimes extended to four. The minister is closely associated with one church, but preaches in all the churches in the Circuit, some of which may have no minister of their own. If certain congregations object to a woman minister the running of the Circuit would be made extremely difficult.[1]

---

[1] The same situation prevails in the United States, but the names vary. The Methodist Church in the United States ordains women to be 'local deacons' and 'local elders' who may serve as 'accepted supply pastors' but cannot be members of Conference. There are 200.

Objections to women preaching are unlikely to be very strong in the Methodist Church which for years has had a considerable number of women among its lay preachers. The objection is rather to a woman assuming leadership in a congregation. In the minds of some Methodists women in the ministry might make a possible future reunion with the Anglican Church more difficult, and they have opposed it on those grounds, while some, especially those who emphasise the Anglican origins of Methodism are, like many Anglicans, convinced that a woman cannot sacerdotally 'represent' the people to God or Christ to His Church. The Methodist Church in Cuba admits women to the order of deacon if they have fulfilled the functions of lay reader satisfactorily for four years and have completed the course of studies. They may then be authorised to administer the Sacraments and conduct marriage services. One woman has been ordained and is the wife of a pastor; five were in the Union Theological Seminary preparing for ordination when the report was written. 'The men are willing,' says the report, 'for women to take country charges.'

There are two United Churches (in which Methodists and Congregationalists have combined) which admit women to the ministry on the same terms as men. One is the United Church of Canada. The first woman was ordained in 1936, and there are now seventeen ordained women. One reason for the ordination of women is suggested in the report as the need of scattered rural areas for somebody, for lack of men, to give the Sacrament and perform marriage services.

The United Church of Christ in Japan, the Kyodan, is mainly Presbyterian, Congregational and Methodist. It was created by State action. Such Anglicans and Lutherans as ever joined it have now withdrawn. There are 103 ordained women in the ministry of the Kyodan—the majority in pastoral work. Although the social environment of Japan is not favourable to the equality of the sexes and only since the war has equal education for boys and girls been a part of the law of the land, yet in the Church the general feeling (except for a non-vocal minority) is that 'all persons are children of God and as such should have equal opportunities to serve Him'. Men tend to be more highly esteemed and to hold more important posts, and women are, of course, limited in what they can do by the claims of home and family, yet the contribution made by the women pastors is really notable and some of them are in charge of congregations. A woman is the minister of one of the largest churches in Tokyo. Many women work with their husbands in a single church or may have two churches in their care. Women are now in a large majority in Japan and have a heavy burden to carry, so that the pastorate of women among other women has great importance.

The discussion of the ministry of women meets with peculiar difficulties in Churches whose church government is Presbyterian. In such Churches the eldership is regarded as a form of ministry and appointment to it is by ordination. Many therefore hold the opinion that if the eldership were opened to women, the ministry must be also, and vice versa.

In Scotland the question of women in the ministry of the Church of Scotland was first raised in 1931 when the Marchioness of Aberdeen presented a petition on behalf of 335 other women asking that the barriers which prevented women from entering the ministry, eldership and diaconate of the Church might be removed. Previously the question had been raised in the Assembly of the United Free Church of Scotland, the presbyteries of Edinburgh, Hamilton, Forres and Nairn together with the presbytery of Manchuria, bringing the matter before the Assembly. It was judged that 'the time was not opportune'. Two years later the Church united with the Church of Scotland. The Duchess of Aberdeen's petition then received attention, and a report on the ministry of women was published with a recommendation that women should be admitted to the diaconate. Hereafter the discussion became one of the admission of women to the diaconate and the eldership, and will be described under that heading. The same situation pertains in the Presbyterian Church in Canada, where women are not admitted either to the eldership or to the ministry. In South Africa in 1944 the Assembly of the Presbyterian Church declared itself 'in favour of the principle of sex equality with regard to the holding of office in the Church and remits the matter to Presbyteries to ascertain the views of the Sessions and Congregations'. Two years later less than ten per cent. of the congregations and less than a third of the Sessions had voted, and in view of the known antipathy in some quarters the matter was dropped by the Assembly. In England the Assembly of the English Presbyterian Church, soon after the first world war, declared 'that there is no barrier in principle to the admission of women to the ministry' and recommended that Churches should use the services of women for preaching. In 1923 it decided that 'it is not the will of the Assembly that the question of admitting women to the regular ministry of the Church should be further considered at the present time', and there are no ordained women in the Church. (This statement followed the admission of women to the eldership in 1922.) In the Presbyterian Churches of the United States women are not admitted to the ministry.

In the Dutch Reformed Church there has been long discussion of the ordination of women. The matter was first raised in and rejected by the Church Synod of 1931. It was again raised in 1946 when the constitutional reform of the Church was under discussion. A strong committee (appointed in 1942) made representations to the commission on constitutional reform, asking for the opening of all the three church offices, of ministry, elder and deacon, to women. The final recommendations for constitutional change in the Church included changes in the ministry, to make for more diversification and a wider range of gifts and functions, but did not include the opening of any part of the revised ministry to women. The word which constantly recurs in Dutch discussion is *regeermacht*—governing power. This power is regarded as being given to the three orders of minister, elder and deacon in the Church. Women by nature and in accordance with Holy Scripture cannot exercise governing power and cannot therefore hold any of these three offices. From time to time bodies of members of the Dutch Reformed Church have broken away from the parent body or have formed religious societies within it. Some of these have united with each other or have rejoined the parent body at a later date, and the picture is confusing for those who are not knowledgable in Dutch Church history. Some of these bodies are more liberal than the parent body, some more fundamentalist, the break being almost always on questions of the interpretation of the Scriptures and on church doctrine. The more fundamentalist bodies do not admit women to church offices, the more liberal do. Among the liberal groups the Vereeniging van Vrijzinnig Hervormden is a society within the Dutch Reformed Church, but it forms its own parishes in certain places where the orthodoxy of the parent church is very strong. This body has women pastors, but in view of the now close association with the Dutch Reformed Church, they do not administer the Sacrament. Another liberal breakaway was the Remonstrantsche Kerk (1619). In this church there have been women pastors since 1915, but in the yearly assembly of 1937 a request was made that the theological seminary should be closed to women at least for the time being. The reason for this is that the church is a very small one, with its membership for the most part among the better educated. From such a community a large number of women sought entry into the theological college, the number then rather exceeding that of the men students. (The total number of ordained men is thirty; women twelve.) Most of the small country churches had women ministers, so that men emerging from college could not find small charges in which to begin their work. Larger churches wanted to have men, so the women in the small churches tended to be stuck where they were, creating a bottle-neck. The result of discussions was that the Church decided to restrict the number of women admitted to the seminary to one third of the number of men students. It also urged that the larger churches should take women assistants and bring about more specialisation between the work of men and women ministers. These regulations are still in operation. This is the only example in the reports of a Church restricting the numbers of women entrants to training because it was getting too many women. The Dutch Lutheran Church, a small minority, is, like the Reformed Church, divided into liberal and fundamentalist groups, the former accepting women in its ministry. The Protestant Church of Indonesia is a united Church, though its strongest links are with the Dutch Reformed Church. Until 1932 it was the State Church of Indonesia. In 1937 the first woman was ordained to its ministry. The extraordinary anomaly therefore exists that Dutch women members of the Dutch Reformed Church with theological qualifications may not hold any office in the Church at home, and if they go abroad are not called missionaries, but 'auxiliaries', yet in the Indonesian Church full ordination is possible.

The situation in regard to the ordination of women is peculiarly elusive in the case of Switzerland because of the different regulations which prevail in the different cantons. The Swiss report says, 'We do not know how many women theologians have so far been ordained in Switzerland.' Something has been said already about the Assistant Ministers, who are theologically trained women. Sometimes these Assistant Ministers perform all the duties of an ordained minister, with the assent of the church authority in the canton, especially in a branch congregation. In Berne, Zurich and Basel (town) the cantonal church constitution allows the Church Council to authorise individual congregations to ordain women as Assistant Ministers. In Soleure the ministry of women was rejected by seven congregations to one in the Synod. In this canton are two independent congregations which have called and ordained women to the full ministry. A number of women assistant ministers are in *de facto* charge of diaspora congregations in Catholic cantons. The Swiss report says that the position of women theologians in Switzerland is becoming 'increasingly unfavourable'. The most favourable time for them was after the first world war.

The Reformed Church of France has for at least twelve years given sustained thought to the question of women in Church and the ministry. It was this Church which asked the World Council of Churches to put the question of the place of women in the Church on the agenda for the first meeting of the Assembly. In 1938 the separate Reformed Churches of France came together to form the Reformed Church of France (E.R.F.). The first Synod of the United Church was held in Lyons in that year. Before this date there had been no joint action by or discussion between the different churches on the work of women. There were already theologically trained women working for the churches. The universities of Paris, Strasbourg and Montpellier were open to women for theological study and a number of French women used to go to the Theological Institute for Women in Geneva.

Among the constituent churches of the United Church the position was as follows:

The Evangelical Reformed Church had already made a place for women as 'pastoral auxiliaries'. This Church gave qualified women a certificate of suitability as deaconess-evangelist. The Reformed Church, without committing itself to any decision in the principle of the ministry of women, did in 1936 give a full pastoral charge to one woman theologian trained at Geneva who worked in a parish in the Department of Lozère.

In the Reformed Church of Alsace the ministry of women has

been accepted for more than twenty years and about ten women are ordained and working in parishes. The writer of the report comments that it might seem strange that this Church, in many ways one of the most conservative of Reformed Churches, should accept the ministry of women. The acceptance had its origin in the terrible devastation of the country in the first world war and the lack of pastors during the twenties. There were already women available who had taken the full theological course at the university of Strasbourg and regulations were made to enable them to work in the parishes. They were to retire on marriage. It was thought best that they should work under the supervision of male pastors, but in actual fact it proved necessary for them to take over smaller parishes. They are commissioned to preach and administer the Sacraments, marry and bury, though in the case of the two latter functions a man is usually called in if he is available.

One of the first tasks undertaken by the newly formed Reformed Church of France, when it met in Synod at Bordeaux in 1939, was to appoint a commission on the ministry of women to survey the field of women's work for the Church and report on it. The war prevented the commission from beginning its meetings until November 1941. Meanwhile, another commission of new members started in the non-occupied zone of France without connection with the Paris group in occupied France.

At every subsequent Synod of the Church reports were received and some action taken. In 1942 the commission decided against the ordination of women to the full ministry of Word and Sacrament, but recommended the Church to explore the possibility of using women's gifts in the parishes. It recommended that the Church should define the conditions of entry into training, the content of training and the terms of service. In 1942 the National Synod at Valence decided to commit the training of younger women for church work to the school opened by the deaconess community in 1941. The general provision was for a two-year course, mainly in Bible study, for women who had reached the age of twenty-five, were either unmarried or widows, and had some occupational or professional training, to whom a diploma would be given permitting them to work for the Church with the understanding that marriage would terminate their service. There are certain special difficulties surrounding the position of women in the Reformed Church of France. The Church is a small one with 600,000 members, scattered unevenly through the country. In some parts they may amount to as much as 80 per cent. of the local population: elsewhere a pastor may have to travel many miles to give the Sacrament to an isolated Protestant family. This makes him of necessity *l'homme à tout faire* in a vast parish, and leaves no room for specialisation in the ministerial function. The report from the vast rural area of the west of France says, 'in a Catholic country the minister is given the aura of a priest . . . country people in the west do, in a confused way, confer on their minister the triple aspect of the priesthood of Christ-prophet, priest and king'. When the elders have accepted a woman as parish assistant acting as pastor, their real thought is summed up in the words 'we said yes because we could not say no'. A further difficulty in France is that all State schools are completely secular-ised and there is therefore no scope for women with theological training in teaching, as there is in Germany, Austria, Great Britain, the countries of the British Commonwealth, and many other countries. It is this fact that has led the Church to insist that women accepted for training in church work shall have some other profession to fall back on.

In recommending that the ministry should not be opened to women the commission, meeting in 1942, went into the question of the nature of the ministry, and the teaching of the Bible on the place of women in the Church. The following is a summary of their main conclusions.

The problem of 'women in the ministry' is really one aspect of the larger question of the nature of the ministry itself in the local church. Obedience to the will of God demands a constant over-haul of church institutions and practices. The New Testament teaches that the Holy Spirit pours out on *the Church* differing marks of grace, and it is the Church which exercises the ministry, and this ministry is made by *charismata*, which complement each other, but over the centuries one type of ministry, the sacerdotal, has eliminated the others from the Church. And now, instead of having a three-fold ministry of ministers of the Gospel, elders and deacons, we have created a monopoly of one ministry aggregating all functions to itself. Therefore it is important to ask what are the essential features of a total ministry of the Church. These are preaching, teaching, the cure of souls and the government of the local Christian community according to the rules of the Church. They all hang together. Yet it is obvious that all these gifts do not appear to the full in one single individual man, and it is in this context that the ministry of women can be rightly talked of.

The commission then goes on to discuss the New Testament teaching, beginning with the text in Galatians 3. 28, 'in Christ there is neither male nor female'. This is the new revelation of life brought to the Church from which the Church has not fully drawn the conclusions. It is dangerous to erect general conclusions valid for all time on the basis of certain texts. The Bible speaks of a subordination of woman to man, not a spiritual subordination, nor one of dignity, nor of ontology, but of function. There is, as it were, a hierarchy of co-ordination. The commission thinks that there is no biblical reason why women should not perform the offices of the full ministry, and some indeed have shown that they can.[1] But they would be reluctant to see women drawn into the one-sided ministry we now possess, so perpetuating what the commission deplores.

The commission goes on to consider the practical side of the question. The function of the ministry is not, they think, such that it can be exercised along with the functions of wife and mother. Public opinion in France is not ready for women pastors, a weighty but not determinative consideration for the Church.

In conclusion, the commission hopes that the Church would not commit itself, except in exceptional cases, to having a woman presiding over the elders of the Church. But they go on to state very strongly that the Church has strayed both from Scripture and from the tradition of the Reformation in making consecration to the pastoral ministry the only consecration recognised by the Church. Neither Scripture nor sixteenth century practice limit consecration in this way, and the ancient discipline of the Reformed Church does not speak of the 'ordination of a pastor', but only of the solemn confirmation of the election of a minister or of the ordination of the ministry. Thus it ought to be considered not only right but indispensable to the Church that women,

---

[1] The reference here would seem to be to pastors' wives who in many instances ran the parishes while their husbands were prisoners of war in Germany.

whose gifts the Church recognises, should be consecrated to the service of God and their fellows by the laying on of hands, such as was used in the Scriptures frequently and in various ways.

In 1949 the Synod of the Reformed Church ruled that in exceptional circumstances the Synod might, on its own initiative and judgment authorise a woman to hold pastoral office. One woman was then confirmed in a pastorate she had held for many years.

The Scandinavian countries, Norway, Sweden and Denmark, have Lutheran State Churches. The clergy of these Churches are appointed by the State (in Sweden a certain number only) and are paid partly by the State which serves as a manager of church funds and imposes taxes in the clerical districts; partly from tithes and old clerical funds. Church affairs are handled by a Ministry of Church Affairs. This arrangement does not mean that the Churches are dictated to by the State in matters of doctrine and Church Order, but it does mean that in certain questions, of which the ordination of women to the priesthood is one, initiative can be taken elsewhere than within the Church itself to bring about changes in Church Order. This has happened in all three countries under review, though the sequence of events has been different in each case. There has been a long and widespread discussion in all three countries about the ordination of women.

In Norway the work of women in home and foreign missionary work has already been noted. For years, however, women were kept back from preaching. After the entry of the Salvation Army in Norway (1890) women began to preach in chapels and camp meetings, but in the churches they had no opportunity to speak on account of legal restrictions. In 1911 Norway was visited by Mrs. Bramwell Booth of the Salvation Army and a well-known preacher (Methodist) from the United States, Miss Anna Snow. The Church authorities were asked to give permission for these two ladies to speak in churches in Oslo and Bergen. Permission was not given and great public discussion arose about the refusal. Organised bodies of women sent resolutions to the Government, including women's political groups, and a number of women doing outstanding voluntary service for the Church supported them. As a result, on December 22nd, 1911, permission was given for women to give religious talks in the churches and take part in the religious teaching of children in the churches. This permission meant that women might not preach over a Bible text. Some years later, February 6th, 1925, this restriction was removed and women were given permission to speak in the churches on the same terms as laymen. But while laymen may preach at statutory services, (July 25th, 1913) such permission is not so far given to women.

After the 1914–18 war, when there was a shortage of pastors, there again arose a demand from women's organisations, this time for the opening of the ministry to women. The main body of Christian opinion in Norway was against any such action by the Government. The Government consulted the bishops, of whom the majority voted against the admission of women to the ministry. The Councils of the Congregations all over the country were in 1926-27 asked to give their point of view and 957 of the 1,000 Councils voted against it. In 200 of the 957 Councils there was not a unanimous vote. Some years later, in 1934, certain members of Parliament put a new proposal before the Government, not directly aimed at the Church, but affecting it. A law of 1912 opened all official positions in the State to women on the same terms as men with some exceptions, including the ministry. The proposal of 1934 was to abolish these restrictions, but it was not carried. It was raised again in 1936, with the same result, but the effect was to stir up public discussion once more, and attention began to be focussed on the number of women of high educational and spiritual standing who were doing voluntary Christian work at home and on the foreign mission field.

In 1936, therefore, the bishops appointed a committee on the 'Work of Women in the Church', with seven members, of whom two were women, and issued their report in the following year. Their plan was to rebuild the old office of deaconess. (In Norway a 'deaconess' has almost always meant a 'nurse'.) The committee recommended (1) that in addition to already existing positions there should be a special form of service for women, and lines were drawn up for such a service; (2) the committee agreed that lay-women should have the same rights in the service of the Church as laymen, i.e. the right to preach and teach and to administer the Sacraments in case of need. The Council of Bishops commented on the report and passed it on to the Ministry for Church Affairs. An interesting feature of the report was that the committee considered seriously the biblical basis of the place of women in the Church. Much had been made in past discussions in the press and elsewhere of St. Paul's dictum that women were to keep silence in the Church. On this matter the committee's report contained the following paragraph:

'The question how far women ought to be used in the service of the Church cannot well be decided by a mere legal plea to the Biblical basis. The question must also to a certain degree be solved on the basis of what contemporary requirements demand. The fundamental point of view of the New Testament concerning the religious equality of women with men has by degrees raised the social position of woman, and made her free to make a higher contribution also in the life of the Church, a contribution she could not possibly have made in the congregation of the early Christian Church.'

On June 24th, 1938, a law was passed through the Norwegian Parliament opening all official positions of the State to women on the same terms as men. This included all the offices of the State Church. A clause, however, was added on the position of women as ministers and pastors which read: 'Women ought not to be given a position as pastor in a congregation if the congregation in question does not want a woman as its pastor.' At the outbreak of war, therefore, the position in Norway was that there was no legal barrier to prevent a woman from being fully ordained as a pastor's assistant, a chaplain to a prison, school or hospital, or, if the congregation expressed a desire for her service, to the full office of parochial ministry. But the problem of women and the pastorates is not solved. If it should happen that one woman really applied for a pastorate and was appointed, the question of ordination would have to be decided by the bishops.

The first woman took a theological degree in Norway in 1899. Between 1928 and 1942 twenty-two women qualified and some of these added the practical course demanded of pastors, so there are women in Norway already fully qualified for the ministry.

War and the invasion of Norway in 1940 put an end to discussion. Women began to play a great part in the work of the Church. Travelling secretaries of Christian organisations served as secret messengers between deported ministers and their parishes. Women came forward readily to run religious meetings, to conduct Bible study, to organise services where opportunity and need arose. Pastors' wives whose husbands were deported or put in prison took up their work as best they could, kept the parish records, administered baptism to new-born children, and kept the congregation together and in good heart.

After the war the bishops took action in response to the action taken by the State, in advance of any particular case being presented to them for decision. They unanimously decided to petition the King to create by order in council a 'lay ministry' (including women), who, if properly qualified, could be consecrated by a pastor according to order from the bishop. As a consecrated 'lay-woman' she could teach and preach, have the pastoral care of women in prison or hospital, administer the Sacraments to sick persons and to congregations in remote areas where the services of a pastor in a church were unobtainable.

A special service for ordination of laymen and women to church work has been drawn up, and in various places in the country courses are held which try to make women fit for service in the congregations.

In Denmark the story of the Church's deliberation upon the subject of women in the ministry and of its relation with the State is different from either that of Norway or Sweden. The writer of the Danish report describes the situation in regard to women's position in society as she sees it. 'On paper we women in Denmark have all that heart could wish. The only difficulty is that one has the feeling from time to time that it is only on paper. It is not that the way is barred to capable women—a woman, for example, is the leading director of one of our largest publishing houses—but it is always the case that it is looked on as an occasion for surprise when a woman occupies a prominent position. It is not yet regarded as natural that a woman should take her part in public life. Consequently her work in the Church is looked on as natural and normal only in so far as she takes on herself the many smaller (but necessary) tasks.'

The question of women in the ministry has been raised in the following way. In the last thirty years some twenty women have taken the same six-years course as the men and hold theological degrees. Of these one has been working since 1929 in a women's prison where she has done a remarkable work in the cure of souls. She herself greatly desired to be able to baptise and to administer the Holy Communion to those who became Christians under her care. Accordingly a group of women theologians brought her case before the College of Bishops, who, on the ground that *in casu necessitatis*, any Christian may exercise these functions, allowed her to do so. Two of the nine bishops would have been prepared to ordain her. Of the rest some objected to the entry of women into the ministry on principle, others thought that the practical objections at the parish level were insurmountable. In February, 1947, all parish councils were asked their opinion on the ordination of women. This had been done twice before and the answer of the majority was always against it.

Such action naturally awakened discussion throughout Denmark. The country had been under German occupation for five years, and there had been little or no contact with other Churches. What other Churches were doing in this matter and what they would think and how the Danish Church's place in the ecumenical movement would be affected by any course of action were all unknown factors.

The most influential opponent of the entry of women into the ministry was the leader of the Danish Fellowship Movement, Pastor Bartholdy, a theologian and church leader in Hasler. His main contention, and that of those who agreed with him, was that on Biblican grounds (I Cor. 14.35; I Tim. 2.12) no woman could be recognised as the ordained leader of divine worship. Many who did not share his theological position felt that the ordination of women would be contrary to Church tradition, which could only be set aside for the weightiest reasons. The followers of Bishop Grundtvig, who formed a recognisable tendency in the Danish Church and carried on the conception of freedom held by their founder, felt that it was an improper compulsion that in this one respect women should not be regarded as full citizens, and they expressed the view that as a matter of simple justice Parliament should by legislative action remove this compulsion. Once this was done it was the Church's own concern to decide what use to make of this freedom. A Danish society for women's rights had been pressing for the removal of the legal barrier to the ordination of women.

In May, 1947, a law was passed in the Danish Parliament, removing the legal barrier to the ordination of women. As seven out of nine Danish bishops were opposed to the ordination of women, and since two women who were ready and desirous of ordination were working in the diocese of a bishop who was opposed to ordination, a second law was passed in the spring of 1948, supplementing the first with a provision that a bishop may refuse to take the oversight of a minister, or woman minister, in his diocese if he chose. Thus Bishop Ølgaard of Odense was free both to ordain and to take the episcopal oversight of two women, one the prison chaplain already mentioned, the other a woman whom a congregation had asked to become its pastor.[1] At the last moment a third woman, who had been appointed as a pastor's assistant in a parish, presented herself for ordination. The three women were ordained together in Odense on April 28th, 1948.

There have been some unexpected sequels to the second of the two Acts of Parliament mentioned. Some of the most vigorous opponents of the ordination of women among the clergy of the Danish Church have asked to be removed from the oversight of Bishop Ølgaard and transferred to the oversight of bishops who have opposed the ordination of women.

The relationship of the Swedish Church to the State is much the same as that of the Norwegian Church to the Norwegian State, but there are factors, both in the development of Swedish society and in the Church situation, which have made the history of discussion and action on the question of women in the ministry markedly different in Sweden.

Sweden has been a pioneer among European countries of social changes making for a high standard of living, a very low birthrate, small families, late marriages and a high proportion of unmarried women and of married women without young children. There is a large number of women free to take a share in public life, and secular women's organisations are powerful. Although their founders were often Christians these organisations have only scanty contact with the Church. Some elements in this secular women's movement have regarded the Church as a conservative force, blocking the way of women's progress. The Church on its side, as in other countries, has been slow to sympathise with women's aspirations and the sympathies of many women are alienated from the Church on this account.

---

[1] In Denmark there is a certain modification in the relationship between Church and State, which allows a voluntary congregation to form itself outside the parish system, but within the Lutheran Church.

The Church of Sweden has a close link with the Anglican Church. Neither Church at the Reformation broke the line of Apostolic Succession, and the Lambeth Conference has recommended that, as in the case of the Church of Finland, intercommunion should be allowed. There is a strong desire in the Church of Sweden not to do anything which might jeopardize this position, and therefore a question which is always raised whenever a change in Church order is contemplated is how such action would be regarded by other Churches within the ecumenical movement, most especially the Anglican Church. The Church of Sweden also has a strong High Church element corresponding somewhat to Anglo-Catholicism in the Anglican Church.

With these facts in mind it is not difficult to see why the discussion of women in the ministry has taken the turn which it has in Sweden in the last twenty or thirty years. An important women's secular alliance, the Fredrika Bremer League, began agitating on this matter more than thirty years ago. Neither Church nor Parliament was insensitive to the position, and in 1919 the Minister of Justice appointed a committee to enquire into the competence of women for government appointments and recommended a legal change which would have opened the ministry. In 1923 a further report recommended the opening of the ministry to women, with some reservations. When the legal barrier was abolished in Norway in 1938, Swedish women's organisations petitioned for a new committee. Early in 1946 a Bill was introduced into the Swedish Parliament for the opening of ministerial orders to women. The Bill was introduced by a prominent clergyman, and there was brisk discussion in the daily press and in church papers.

In August, 1946, the Church called together a conference at Sigtuna, where theologians and Church leaders discussed the matter, and suggested a new office for women, allowing them to exercise pastoral care and preach. Meanwhile, a Parliamentary Committee was appointed to work on the subject. It was presided over by Bishop Bohlin of Härnosand. The discussions were long and thorough, and in March, 1949, the committee reported back to Parliament, eleven members being in favour of the ordination of women and four against. The Report of the Commission contained a recommendation that 'Women shall have the same right as men to obtain ordination and to hold ministerial office;

but women may not obtain appointments in parishes where there are not at least two ministerial posts, at least one being occupied by a man. With regard to other kinds of Church service than the ordained ministry, women shall have equal rights with men'. Meanwhile the Synod of the Church had made it quite clear that it will not countenance the ordination of women. Even if the group within the Church, which includes many of the leading Swedish Church women, succeeds in carrying the Church with it in its advocacy of a special ministry for women, it is very doubtful whether the State would countenance such an order or allow money for the salaries of any women ordained into it.

At this moment, therefore, the Swedish Church faces not only the possibility of a protracted argument with the State and perhaps a clash with secular movements, both of which might be serious enough, but it is also faced with the possibility of real division amongst its own members. There are within the Church strongly conservative forces which take quite literally the prohibition of St. Paul on women speaking or holding authority in the Church. There are elements which place strong emphasis on Church tradition. There is another section working for the entry of women into the full office of the ministry, and there is the already mentioned section of opinion working for a new branch of the ministry.

In making comparisons with the situation in other Churches it is important to bear in mind that classical Lutheran theology does not accept the conception of three orders of ministry, but holds the view that there is only one, though that one may have a number of branches. Disputes about this among the clergy add to the difficulty of the present situation.

The Church of Sweden has very few posts to offer to women. Those who have taken a degree in theology, with one exception, teach in schools. However, the Women's Council, started in 1948 with the blessing of the Bishops' Conference, opened a combined retreat house and training centre, and while the controversy goes on about full ordination or none, a small body is working steadily to train women for special service in the Church.

It will be realised that the discussion of the training, position and work of the Vikarinnen in the previous chapter covers a good deal of the same ground as any discussion of the ordination of women in Germany and Austria might be expected to cover, for it is over the position of the Vikarinnen that the matter is raised.

In 1941 and 1942 a commission of theologians was appointed in the Confessional Church in Germany to discuss the theological foundations of the office of Vikarin. It was presided over by Professor Ernst Wolf and contained three women. 'These discussions,' wrote one of the women members, 'were most fruitful. They took us to the fundamentals. They brought out the essential character of the New Testament ministry as *diakonia* and showed the close connection between evangelistic service of the Gospel and the actual personal attitude and associations of the individual. All legal and casuistical questions were shown to be open to question. But it was curious that after that no agreement could be reached as to practical deductions. We women had the impression that with some of the men the preconceptions which they brought to this Bible study remained unchanged. So to our sorrow it turned out that there could be no real understanding between the theological leaders of the Confessional Church.' Later the Evangelische Frauenarbeit in Deutschland invited a group of theologians to discuss the place of the woman theologian in the Church.

The generally prevailing opinion in the Church in Germany is that women cannot be fully ordained but may be commissioned as Vikarinnen to special tasks. The debate is about the status of the Vikarin which varies from province to province, and the functions she may perform. But the debate also includes the whole question of the place of women in the Church and there are some theologians who argue that the grounds which exclude women from the ministry exclude them also from the right to vote for a representative to any church body. 'On the other hand,' says the German report, 'there are theologians in the Confessional Church who acknowledge the authority of the *theologia relevata* and base upon it their readiness to accept the service of women in the official ministry of the Church. They argue that the preaching of God's Word both by men and by women has authority only in so far as it is confirmed by the Holy Spirit . . .' Thus a leading superintendent minister in Berlin, a strong Calvinist, is in favour of the ministry of women in the parishes, and others also, meeting in small groups, have subjected the extreme conservative view of the place of women in the Church to searching criticism. 'The younger generation of theologians who almost everywhere have formed themselves into small societies do not share the views expressed by the older clergy because at the time of the Church struggle under the Nazis men and women students and the young assistant ministers of the Confessional Church, bound together by the same dangers and the same loyalties, learned to value each other.'

One would expect to find that theological debate on the matter of the ordination of women would be at its strongest in Germany, and this is certainly so. Yet even the most implacable opponent of women's ordination has the authority of Luther himself for saying that in times of emergency it is better that a woman should preach than that the Word of God should be without a preacher. In many places a compromise was made with circumstance and women Vikarinnen assumed the full office of the ministry during the war. German clergy were subject to military conscription along with all other male citizens. Many were killed in the war, and throughout the war period the training of clergy was at a standstill. Women who were qualified and able to do so began to take over the neglected work of some of the parishes. Now only two or three women remain in charge of parishes in the West, and almost all the provincial church authorities in the West have narrowed the field of activity for women. In the East the reverse is the case, and arising out of the work they did during the war women continue to hold pastoral positions in the Church. The reason both for the expansion in the East and the retraction in the West is the same—the flight of clergy from East to West, leaving parishes in the East without pastors, and bringing into the West a large body of married men with families for whose livelihood the Church was responsible. As soon as women were not needed theological arguments against their ministry were strongly voiced in the Church.

There is no more overpowering answer to the question whether, leaving for the moment on one side the theological issue, women are *able* to exercise the full ministry, if they are given the opportunity, than the account in the German report of the work of a number of Vikarinnen in the East of Germany in the last part of the war and since. When the married pastors left for the Reich, these women stayed behind as the Russian armies advanced. Breslau was heavily besieged, and two Vikarinnen and nine pastors were all the spiritual help left in a great city. The women worked in the camps for refugees who had come into the city from Warsaw and Lodz, and one of them was wounded in the siege. Another woman in Silesia who had been engaged in women's work was put in charge of a church, from which the pastor had fled without the approval of the church authorities, and stayed with the parishioners and was evacuated with them by the Russians. Two other Vikarinnen in Silesia acted as wandering women preachers. When the Russians sent all the pastors out of Upper Silesia, one of these women remained with the parish to which she had just been appointed and was captured and imprisoned for four months by the Russians. Disguised as a Polish peasant woman with a shawl on her head and a bundle on her back and with bare feet, she succeeded in crossing the boundary and moved from village to village conducting services. The other of these two looked after little congregations in fifty villages and so well organised her work that by spending a day in each place she was able to conduct church business, marriages, baptisms, classes for confirmation and church services. Yet another woman whose husband was a pastor and was in the war, sent her children into the Reich and carried on the parish until she and the parishioners were evacuated. Another woman who took charge of a parish found that the leadership of the pastoral council often fell to her lot. There was a great spiritual reawakening in the distresses of this terrible time of defeat and Russian occupation and, said one of the Vikarinnen, 'people no longer enquired who preached God's Word to them: they were only concerned that they should hear it at all'. Nor were these Vikarinnen the only ones who showed what women are able to do when the opportunity comes to them. Several of them in other parts of Germany than Silesia were directed by the Gestapo to exhausting munition work and yet continued to hold classes and services in the evenings and on Sundays to the limit of their strength.

The situation in Austria has been very much the same. As the clergy were called up to war service, so the Vikarinnen were called upon by the Church to preach and to take charge of distant congregations. Only one woman had full charge of a parish, but others shared in large parishes the work of the minister, and one, attached to the leading church in Vienna, found her work in the scattered congregations in the mountains. 'The outward circumstances of such services are simpler and more poverty-stricken than one can imagine. A few Protestants in the midst of an over-powering Roman Catholic majority come together once a month. They have no house of God. During the war the State no longer allowed them the use of the schoolroom. So the Roman Catholic parish priest frequently placed a church or chapel at their disposal. I can certainly say that I have more often held a service in a Roman Catholic than in a Protestant church.' There had been nothing to compare in Austria with the theological debate in Germany, but the effect of the work of the Vikarinnen was to create a small minority 'mostly of the ministers who had had Vikarinnen as regular colleagues, who were in favour of the full ministry of women'. All the Vikarinnen were young, the oldest thirty-six and the youngest twenty-nine, but although their first appearance in a congregation was met with some reserve, the congregations were sorry to see them go when the Church with-drew its permission for this enlargement of their work at the end of the war. One, after strong representations had been made by her parish for the retention of her services, was allowed to remain by special dispensation.

In the Anglican Church the order of deaconesses is 'the one existing order of ordained ministry for women'. This has been dealt with in the section on deaconesses rather than here, in order to treat under one heading those who in the different Churches carry the same name. The ordination of women, and the work which trained and dedicated women could do for the Church, has been the subject of very careful study in the Church of England for more than thirty years. As has already been shown, the order of deaconesses was revived in a practical sense when the Bishop of London made Elizabeth Ferard a deaconess in 1862, but from then on each bishop acted in the matter as he saw fit, ordaining women or licensing deaconesses to work within his diocese. There was no recognised status or prescribed functions. In 1917 the Archbishop of Canterbury appointed a committee on the ministry of women. Its report published in 1919 contained a detailed historical survey of the order of deaconesses and recom-mended its revival. In the following year the Lambeth Conference (all the bishops of the Anglican Communion throughout the world, meeting in a consultative capacity), recommended that the order of deaconesses should be revived throughout the Anglican Communion. In England the order of deaconesses was formally restored by the Convocation of Canterbury in 1923 and of York in 1925. In 1930 the Lambeth Conference again returned to the matter. There was considerable doubt and uncertainty about what the order of deaconesses was. Confusion was caused by the fact that the order of deacon in the Church of England is, in the words of a subsequent Archbishops' Commission, 'commonly treated as being little more than a relatively brief apprenticeship for the priesthood'. Those who opposed the opening of the full ministry to women were therefore asking whether the order of deaconesses was secretly regarded by those who favoured it as a first step in a process designed to end with women in the priesthood. Those who wanted to secure for women an ordination equal to that of. men but different from it were asking whether the order, with its doubtful status and restricted functions, was to be permanently equated with a form of ordination which for men was superseded by ordination to priesthood in a couple of years. Were women ordained as deaconesses to be regarded as being 'in Holy Orders'? The Lambeth Conference of 1930 said that the Order of deaconesses was 'an Order *sui generis* . . . which both from the solemnity of its ordination and the importance of its functions can satisfy the fullest desires of women to share in the official work of the Church'. 'We have to make up our minds,' said the Archbishop of Canterbury, 'that the status we give them is that of women who are ordained, who are in Orders. If there is some hesitation to use the term "in Holy Orders" it was largely due to the legal position which the phrase "a person in Holy Orders" involves. But we must make it quite clear that once and for all we regard these women as being an Order within the Church to which they are solemnly ordained.' However, the process of getting the position of the deaconesses recognised by bishops, clergy and people as an order of ministry is one very far from complete.

Following the Lambeth Conference of 1930 the Archbishops of Canterbury and York appointed another Commission on the ministry of women. It was a powerful body containing as it did five bishops and the Dean of St. Paul's, as well as a few eminent theologians and four women. The Commission received reports and interviewed many witnesses and its report was published in 1935. The Commission went very thoroughly into the theological arguments presented to them by witnesses for and against the ministry of women. These included the lack of any indication of a general priesthood open to women in the Bible, the fact that Christ was a man and can only be represented by a man, that in the Godhead there is a subjection of one person to another without loss of equality. 'The witnesses who have adduced theological or semi-theological arguments have not convinced us' wrote the Commission in their report, 'that in these matters a full settlement of the whole matter is to be found.' They rejected the entry of women to the three orders of ministry in the following terms, 'While the Commission as a whole would not give their positive assent to the view that a woman is inherently incapable of receiving the grace of Order, and consequently of admission to any of the three Orders, we believe that the general mind of the Church is still in accordance with the continuous tradition of a male priesthood. It is our conviction that this consensus of tradition is based upon the will of God and is, for the Church today, a sufficient witness to the guidance of the Holy Spirit.' The Commission further added that while it would be, in its opinion, within the right of a re-united Church to make such a change as the admission of women to the three orders of ministry, it was not a step which one branch of the Church could rightly take in isolation. The Report went on to make recommendations about the order of deaconesses and about the lay work of women. While it could not equate the order of deaconesses with any of the three orders for men, 'we nevertheless think that it is among the clergy and not among the laity that the deaconess should be ranked'.

Yet another Archbishop's committee was appointed in 1942 and reported in 1943. It surveyed the whole field of women's work for the Church and gave careful scrutiny to the way in which the order of deaconesses was functioning. Lack of recruitment gave cause for concern and it was proposed by the committee that the age should be lowered from thirty to twenty-five, on the ground that most women know by that age what they want to do with their lives.

It will be seen from what has been said that the Anglican Communion sets great store by the tradition of the past and by the unity of the action of the Church, that is to say, it regards the ordination of women to the ministry as a matter of principle and does not use the method of licensing women to perform ministerial functions without ordination to the full ministry. In a country district in China where the people were without a pastor the

Bishop of Hong Kong gave permission to a deaconess to act as priest. The standing committee of the Hong Kong diocese then brought a resolution to the General Synod of the Chung Hwa Sheng Kung Hui (the Anglican Church in China) that a new Canon should be added to the Canons of that Church permitting, for an experimental period of twenty years, the ordination of suitable women to the priesthood. The Synod referred the matter to the Lambeth Conference, then about to meet, in the form of a question which asked 'whether or not such liberty to experiment within the framework of the Anglican Communion would be in accordance with Anglican tradition and order'. The reply of the Lambeth Conference was that such liberty of experiment in so profound a matter would not be in accordance with Anglican tradition and reaffirmed the 1930 resolution on the order of deaconesses.

It remains to give some account of what ordained women themselves think of their work out of the personal records collected together in some of the reports. All are conscious of being in one sense or another 'on trial' in the Church. They are realists about their position. Even in Churches where the ordination of women is of long standing and they have won their place among their fellow ministers, they know that this acceptance is not accorded so readily in the congregations. 'We'd rather have had a man that warn't so good,' remarked an old American farmer, after some quite appreciative remarks about a woman minister. Women ministers know that this is often the case, and their ministry usually begins and often continues to be among the small congregations of the countryside where opinions are conservative but are over-ridden by the state of the church's bank balance. So the woman minister is not tested solely on her powers of preaching and her understanding as a pastor: she often goes to a place where she must either set the business affairs of the church forward, or inspire confidence in others to do it for her. The American report quotes a number of instances where women ministers have built up a church from tiny beginnings and have launched out with success on the building of larger premises and the raising of money. Another fact which women ministers know quite well is that they are not going to find it easy to move to another congregation when they feel that the time has come. One woman who has been in a rather large church for some time and has held positions in her denomination never before accorded to a woman, remarks that in her own church prejudice has quite faded and in all the surrounding churches she is an often invited and warmly welcomed visitor, but that she knows that every one of the churches would, if the question of her becoming their minister were raised, have a minority in opposition which would make the appointment impossible. Another fact on which women comment is that they must be in preaching and in all other parts of the minister's work well above the average to be regarded as even moderately good. 'If I were to preach half as badly as some of my fellow ministers I should be in difficulties!' comments one.

There are very few examples of married women carrying on a pastorate, except as assistants to their husbands, and women ministers seem to accept the usual ruling of Churches that women must resign on marriage as reasonable and right. Many women as widows of ministers even with little training have made a success of pastoral work because of the experience gained as ministers' wives. One or two comment on the difficulty which a woman experiences when she is in a position where she has to act in a civic capacity. One French woman, for example, found herself having to conduct the public funeral of a number of air-raid victims. On the other hand, women ministers comment that they find that they are the recipients of many confidences, especially domestic ones, that they are able to help with troubles with children, that once the strangeness has worn off there are not noticeably fewer men in their congregations than in most others, and that they are often more loyally backed by men lay representatives than a man minister because it is felt that they need this support.

No life has less glamour, less chance of a career, poorer financial reward or more hard work. Yet women write of their work with great affection, saying that there is no other reason for doing it than the inner irrepressible conviction that they are being called by God and cannot do anything else. Women who have been compelled by changes in church law to give up the pastoral work they did during the war speak of the loss of it with grief.

The ministry of women directly affects only a very tiny minority of women in the Church, whether one looks at the number who are actually ordained or at those who might want to be if the situation in their Church were different. It is no slight upon the service of these women to their own Churches to say that the most important part about the discussion of the ministry of women has been its indirect influence. The raising of the question 'should women be ministers?' has compelled those charged with answering it to re-examine the nature of the ministry, and without exception all Churches which have seriously discussed the question of women in the ministry have also had to look to the broader aspect of the place of *all* women in the Church.

V

THE PARTICIPATION OF WOMEN IN THE
GOVERNMENT OF THE CHURCH

THIS SECTION is concerned with the share that women take
in the government of the Churches, local, regional and
national. This might seem on the face of it to be the easiest
matter, involving only a single question 'How far do women
possess the rights that men possess in this matter?' But to define
and describe the rights of laymen in the government of their
Churches would be exceedingly difficult. Nearly all the Churches
dealt with in this book are ancient institutions whose customs
have grown with them. Even new Churches are offshoots of, or
breakaways from, older Churches, and have retained some of the
features of their parents. Offices therefore exist in the Churches
which were created in times when the functions of the lay officers
of a congregation included much that is now considered the work
of other bodies than the Church. On the other hand, Churches
now have functions not thought of in bygone ages. Thus a series
of changes have taken place. Ancient offices have often been
retained and the functions modernised, or these offices may survive as names and even as honourable titles, but without much of
the substance of authority in them. Corporate groups holding
office in the Church may also have undergone change, or it may
be found that although a certain governing body may be considered as a part of Church order, its functions are slender
compared to those of some quite modern committee or council in
the Church in which many of the day-to-day decisions may be
taken. In other words, it is extremely difficult to tell precisely
where power lies in the affairs of the Churches, nor is there any
ecumenical study of the lay offices of the Churches to which the
reader may be directed for information.

One general comment can be made. The most ancient lay offices in the Church tended to be individual offices—that of churchwarden in the Church of England, to give a classic example. After the Reformation one begins to see the emergence of corporate responsibility—the kirk session, for example, and the deacons' meeting of the Congregational and Baptist local Churches, which is corporately responsible for the Churches' affairs. Some of the Churches which arose out of the Reformation, especially those in which Calvin's influence was strong, developed a strongly democratic pattern. The ultimate authority in the Church was for them the whole body of believers, who delegated the taking of executive decisions and certain spiritual functions in the congregation to elected representatives corporately responsible to the congregation. The diaconate of a Church of the Reformed tradition is not the sum of individual officers each responsible for one task or holding one office: it is a corporate entity and responsibility and authority are vested in the group. This principle, together with certain methods of procedure in the running of a group democracy were handed on by these Churches to political and social institutions, where they mingled with other democratic forces stemming from secular liberalism and humanism to form the Western democratic tradition. It is not possible to say that Churches of this kind directly influenced Churches based on the hierarchical principle and made them more democratic, but democratic ideas in society have certainly caused such Churches to make room for democratic practices within a framework expanding with the times. New boards, councils, assemblies, or whatever they were called, grew up within or alongside of existing church order. These made room for women both as electors and as members. It is almost universally true to say that wherever a Church has modified its constitution or its practice in the direction of forming new bodies to which it has delegated certain powers, women have found themselves accepted almost without question. But for women to gain access to the more ancient lay offices and lay boards of the Churches, when these have been for centuries the monopoly of men, is a much more difficult and much slower process.

Unfortunately the World Council questionnaire did not ask whether women could vote for the membership of governing boards in Churches. This is a question usually settled before women reach the point of standing for election. There are still countries in which the vote is an undecided issue, and others where the battle is not quite such ancient history as to have been entirely forgotten. The Scottish report, for example, speaks of the history of the women's vote for male office bearers. 'The first trace of a women's vote occurs in a secession congregation in Kinclaven in 1747.' As the century went on it came to be understood that among the Burghers the female vote passed unchallenged, while among the anti-Burghers it was disallowed. In 1821 in the Presbytery of Wigtown the question of women voters was first raised in the United Church. In 1856 it was announced that all members in full communion had a right to vote in the election of office bearers. 'But in 1843 two lay members of the Free Church summoned a meeting on the subject and spoke emphatically against the idea as contrary to the very essence of the Church of Scotland as a Spiritual Church.' Their views coincided with those of certain German theologians quoted in the last chapter who regard the vote as an exercise of power from which women are by their sex excluded.

In Switzerland (the only country in Europe and one of the few in the world where women have no political vote) the position of women varies from canton to canton. In many cantons the Church is still tied to the State by law, and changes are therefore difficult to make. In Berne, the Grisons, Soleure, Schwyz and Basel (town) women have the right to vote in the Church and also to sit in councils. In Ticino they have the vote. In Aargau and Thurgau individual Churches are free to grant women the vote if they wish to do so: none have. In some cantons the matter has been the subject of debate for years. In Zurich, for example, the matter was first raised in 1902 and intermittent discussion has gone on ever since. The Synod voted for the right of church suffrage to be extended to women in 1932 and forwarded its resolution to the Cantonal Council. When a plebiscite was taken in 1947 the proposal suffered overwhelming defeat. The Swiss report closes with some interesting observations on a situation which must occasion surprise to those who think of Switzerland as Europe's oldest democracy and remember her long battle in the cause of freedom. 'The one-sided development of the Church in Switzerland has made it difficult for many live and gifted women to work within it. We are still living today on a tradition (as far as the Church is concerned) which, however, we can no longer hand on to our children unless we succeed in building up a new and living relationship between women and the Church. Both in the Church authorities, and among women, people are beginning to realise this. In our opinion the lowest point in this relationship has now been passed, but the question needs much more serious attention and much more honest goodwill from both sides.'

In the great majority of Churches, however, it is now taken for granted that women have the power to vote for representatives to serve the local congregation, even if they are not able to vote for the higher authorities in the Church. It is not at all easy to distinguish between a situation in which they may serve if elected but in fact do not come forward for election, from one in which they are expressly forbidden to serve. Churches do not tend to parade anti-feminist feeling and the forces which keep women off governing boards are often psychological—the women themselves know that they just would not be accepted—rather than legal.

The simplest way of trying to lay out a comparison between the practice of the different Churches in this matter is to treat first Europe, then America and then the newer Churches of the East and of Africa, treating the Churches of the countries of the British Commonwealth with the mother Churches which they so very strongly resemble. Two hundred years of separation has been enough to cause different traditions to grow up in some matters, as between for example German and American Lutheranism, Methodism as it exists in Great Britain and in the United States, and terms are not used within single confessions in exactly the same sense in different countries.

It was pointed out in an earlier chapter that for Churches with a presbyterian form of government great difficulties arise about the appointment of women because the eldership is regarded as a form of ordination. In some Churches the diaconate also is regarded as an ordained office in the Church. The Churches in Scotland have a divided history in this matter. 'In the Free Church deacons are ordained and therefore women are not allowed to sit in the deacons' courts. In the pre-union United Free Church women were admitted to the diaconate in 1919 and it was expressly stated at the time that this was not on the basis of ordination. In 1934 the General Assembly of the Church of Scotland agreed that women were eligible for the diaconate on the same terms as men. Since then numbers have served in the deacons' courts in the congregations. The United Free Church Continuing threw open the diaconate, eldership and ministry to women in 1929, a favourable vote being obtained both in the Assembly and in the presbyteries when the matter was submitted to them.' The question of the eldership presents far greater difficulties. As has been said, a petition was sent in the name of five presbyteries to the Assembly in 1926. In 1931, two years after the Union, the matter was raised again by the Marchioness of Aberdeen's petition. It led to a commission which recommended the opening of the diaconate to women. This was done. The question of the eldership was discussed in the presbyteries and a majority favoured the opening of the eldership to women. The 1944 General Assembly accepted an overture to this effect and in accordance with legal requirements sent the matter again to the presbyteries. Again they approved. But the General Assembly of 1945 decided that the matter must be again submitted to the presbyteries with the instruction that they should ascertain the views of the Kirk Sessions and the Congregations. The vote then turned in the opposite direction. The Scottish report remarks that there is no doubt that the matter really turns on one function of the elder, that of carrying the elements from the Holy Table to the members of the congregation in the Communion Service. Should women be allowed to do this? But in making up their minds on this matter, while members of the Assembly may perhaps think in terms of the meaning of the ministry and the nature of church order, many people in the congregations are moved by such considerations as whether having women elders will cause men to despise the office, and inability to imagine what a woman elder would properly wear. Indeed, women suffer very often from the variety of their dress, with its stress on individuality. Men, and even more women, cannot see a woman in a representative rôle.

The Scottish report goes on to mention the fact that the exclusion of women from the regular offices of the Church and from membership of the higher courts has helped the growth of something like dual control. The General Assembly works through committees, some of which have great influence. Women sit on most of these and one woman has been a sub-convener. At the level of the presbytery and of the local congregation there is also an increasing tendency to work through committees, and on these women have served with acceptance and made a contribution which 'continually calls in question the rightness of their continued exclusion from the eldership and the traditional courts of the Church'.

In the Dutch Reformed Church women are excluded both from the eldership and from the diaconate. It is a practice in a few places for women to be invited to serve as sub-deacons: as such they share in the charitable work of the deacons and attend meetings but without vote. This is done independently by the minister and not by the ruling of the authoritative body of the Church. In the liberal offshoots of the Reformed Church women serve in the diaconate, and in the Dutch Lutheran Church women serve as deacons and as elders. As in Scotland, but not to the same extent, a good deal of power resides in committees which make suggestions to the Synod on policy, and some women sit on these committees, to which they have been appointed by the Synod. Women also serve on certain interdenominational boards, provided always that they do not hold 'governing power', the phrase on which in Holland the question of women in the Church so largely turns.

In the Reformed Church of France women have been eligible for membership of presbyterial councils for some years. The writer of the report thinks that women have gained this right for the good work that they have done, but that there are men who are anxious to keep women at a distance for fear that a parish should become 'a company of women round the pastor'.

In the Reformed Church of Hungary 'there are no women among our Church authorities', says the report. It then goes on to quote from the church constitution that if 'women fulfil the requirements of eligibility they may serve as church councillors, professors, teachers, deaconesses, distributors of tracts, guardians of orphans and the poor and members of charitable and social committees, but they are not eligible for other offices of the Church'. In certain towns with a large population of members of the Reformed Church (80–90 thousand in one case) there is only one large church session which may consist of as many as 100 members. But the local communities have their own councils and in these councils women serve as well as men. A suggestion that the regional communities should have their own church government has now been made, and unless the church constitution were changed women would not be allowed to sit on the church sessions which the new arrangement would bring into every community.

In Czechoslovakia women have equal rights with men in the Czechoslovak Church (its constitution dates from 1920). In the Czech Church of the Brethren women have the vote and also serve in the presbyteries, but not in the higher courts of the Church.

In the Lutheran Churches of Sweden, Norway, Denmark and Finland women serve on the local boards of the congregations. The right was given to women in Denmark in 1903. In Sweden women are not members of the official board of the diocese, known as the Chapter, but they serve on the diocesan council and are at the national level eligible for membership of the Church Congress, composed of clergy and laity. The total number of members is sixty, of which two were women when the report was written. In Finland there are no women in governing boards above the local level. The Norwegian report remarks that the number of women on local boards and diocesan councils is small, but their contribution is valuable because they are the outstanding women of the Christian community.

In Germany theological opinion on the part which women may play in the laity of the Church is as divided as opinion on women in the ministry. 'It is usually admitted that women can be elected to the parish church councils and to the Synods of the Landeskirchen, but very few are to be found there. There are no women in the governing bodies of the Landeskirchen. In the parish councils there are more women in the West than in the East and in the cities than in the villages. A few women have been elected to the Synods of the Landeskirchen, but many Synods have no women. There appear to be more women in official capacities than in elected capacities, thus the legal adviser to the Consistory of the Church in Berlin is a woman, and so is the legal adviser to the Evangelische Kirche in Deutchland (E.K.D.) and even theological advisers are in some cases women. The E.K.D. is governed by a Council of 12 members and an Assembly of 120. In the former there are no women and in the latter 4, of whom one was elected by the Synod of her Landeskirche and the other three were appointed by the council of the E.K.D. There is no mention in the constitutions of any church bodies of women's rights either to vote or to be elected.'

In England women participate in the government of all the Churches. All the lay offices of the Baptist, Congregational and Methodist Churches are open to women. It is quite impossible to tell from the report in how many local congregations women are not accepted, just from custom: probably the war, removing all but the older men, made women's co-operation essential. In the Methodist Church women have been eligible as members of Conference since 1911, the vice-chairman of Conference must always be a lay person and has twice been a woman. Among the 26,000 lay preachers, 2,000 are women, and as Class leaders women are in a majority. The eldership of the English Presbyterian Church was opened to women in 1922. The Church of England underwent a large-scale change of its form of government in 1919. The two Convocations remained the supreme authority in matters of doctrine and the discipline of the Church, but by an Enabling Act passed through Parliament in that year, control of nearly all other aspects of the Church's life, including much that had previously needed parliamentary action, passed into the power of a National Assembly of the Church of England (usually called the Church Assembly). The Act also empowered the Church to set up elected bodies in the parishes, the rural deaneries and the dioceses, to deal with church affairs, and it was expressly stated that the laity must be represented in these bodies and may be represented by either men or women. The Church Assembly consists of three houses—of Bishops, Clergy and Laity. Deaconesses are not accepted by opinion in the Church at large as members of the clergy and do not sit in the House of Clergy, but there are 83 women in the 330 lay members elected in 1950 for a term of five years. The number was slightly higher in the previous Assembly. It is not too much to say that the parochial church councils have transformed the life of the parishes. Many of the duties which formerly fell to the incumbent of the parish or to the churchwardens now rest upon the parochial church council. The incumbent is *ex officio* chairman, and while it is true that there are a few places where he has done everything to prevent the council from operating, on the whole the partnership between ministry and laity at the level of the local church has been immensely strengthened. Women are playing a full part in these parochial church councils, sometimes serving as secretaries. By the same Act the office of churchwarden was also opened to women and they have served as such in some churches. Women have also been elected as lay representatives to the diocesan conferences. The Church of Ireland and the Church of Wales are disestablished Churches and were unaffected by the Enabling Act. In the Church of Wales all lay offices are open to women. In the Church of Ireland they may serve at the local level but not in the higher courts of the Church. In the Methodist Church of Ireland and in the Presbyterian and Methodist Church in Wales women may serve on all boards. It should perhaps be pointed out that one of the reasons why women serve in the representative bodies of all the Churches in England is undoubtedly the general acceptance of women in the social life, and particularly in the local government, of the country. For more than 70 years women have served in local government as elected councillors and committee members: hundreds have been mayors and magistrates. It has not therefore been necessary for the Churches to pioneer in finding women capable of handling business or men ready to accept their participation willingly.

The countries of the British Commonwealth share the religious tradition of Great Britain and there is very little variation in the pattern of church life. In New Zealand it appears that although the liberty to serve is almost the same as in England there is less participation of women in church government. The Baptist Church, for example, reports that women may serve as deacons in some congregations, but that this is not general. In the Presbyterian Church the eldership of women has not been accepted in the presbyteries and is not therefore permitted by the Church, though they serve as deacons and as managers (trustees). 'Actually,' says the New Zealand report, 'very few women are appointed to church courts. The Anglican communion is behind England in this respect. There are not many women on parish vestries, and men are sent as lay representatives to the Synods, except that in one diocese a deaconess sits as a layman. In other communions the situation is much the same.'

The position of women in Australia would appear to be midway between England and New Zealand. Four dioceses admit women as members of the synod in the Anglican Church. They may be members of parochial councils. Membership of all boards of the Methodist Church is open to them, but they are not allowed to act as trustees in a circuit. 'In most denominations there is an increasing desire to see women take an equal share with men in the management of the Church, but women are often just as opposed to this as men are. Opposition is not always open; it shows itself through the ballot.'

In South Africa the Presbyterian Church has recently turned down a proposal that women should be eligible as elders. They serve on the boards of management which look after the property of the local congregation and on other committees, local and regional. In the Anglican Church they may serve as churchwardens and sidesmen, and a move for them to be eligible for provincial assemblies is expected to succeed. In the Methodist Church there is equality of men and women in all lay representative offices. In the Dutch Reformed Church women have no share in the government of the Church but serve on many social committees.

An example of the low social estate of women being reflected in the Church is furnished by the brief report from the Baptist Church in Italy. In some congregations, far from occupying any place in the government of the Church, women's names are not allowed to appear in the list of subscribers to church funds, anything they give being attributed to their husbands.

Of the Orthodox Churches it may be said that the form of government is so different that comparisons with Churches which have been influenced by western conceptions of democracy are very difficult to make. As has already been said, the work of the Church in Greece is all carried out under the bishops, and women take their share in the work of committees, especially for social work. In the Russian Orthodox Churches which have sprung up in many places outside Russia where Russians have settled, women play a very large part in keeping the parishes going, although their participation is hardly formalised in rules. They assist the priests, sometimes in the actual worship, and always in the charitable work of the parish which is very heavy among a community with no other home than its Church, and they assist also in the business management of the parishes. In Russia itself the terms on which the Church has been allowed to survive have been severe. By law no congregation may be recognised unless twenty persons will stand as sponsors and take the financial burden of the Church on their shoulders. This is often heavy because of the high

rate of taxation, yet for men acceptance of this responsibility with
its open alliance with the Church may mean loss of livelihood. So
women have come forward and undertaken the task and it is
largely thanks to them that many of the congregations of the
Orthodox Church survive in Russia today. 'They not only do the
hard work of cleaning and heating the churches, but they appear
before the authorities as the witnesses of a forbidden religion.'

The report from the United States contains in an appendix a
tabulated return showing the legal status of women in 105 denominations. Seventy-one of these give women a share in the
government of the local church, thirty-three do not, and in one
the practice varies from diocese to diocese.

The great majority of the Churches in the United States are of
European origin: a minority of Churches are American in origin
and have a separate existence from Europe, and divisions and
mergers have made for variations.

In the Baptist and Congregational Churches women may share
in the work of governing the Church locally (though this varies
between local churches) and denominationally. In the Southern
Baptist Convention, a very large and in many respects conservative Church, there seems to be no place for women locally
although they sit in the highest assembly of the Church. The
larger of the Congregational bodies has a ruling that one third of
the members of national boards and of the biennial meetings of
the General Council must be women. This Church reports that
about one-tenth of its local churches have women deacons. But
'for Congregational, Disciple and American Baptist Churches, the
question whether deaconesses are equal to deacons can only be
answered by a person knowing a given local church. They may
meet with the deacons and share in certain of their tasks; again
they may not. Rarely, certainly, do deaconesses serve the Lord's
Supper as the deacons do' (by serving the Lord's Supper is meant
carrying the elements from the minister's hands to the people,
who remain in their seats). Two women have held the office of
President of the American Baptist Convention. The Congregational Christian General Council elected a woman moderator in
1948. Seven Presbyterian Churches are listed. The largest of
these, the Presbyterian U.S.A. admits women both as deacons and
as elders, but their functions differ from church to church; in
some they are allowed to serve the Lord's Supper and in others they

are not. One of the matters of church order in which the Presbyterian churches are divided is the admission of women to the
diaconate and eldership. The Presbyterian Church U.S., the
second largest body, will not admit women either as deacons or
as elders, though women have served on national boards since
1924. Thirty per cent. of the Presbyterian U.S.A. churches which
replied said that they had women deacons. The proportion of
women among the elders is much smaller, and for this reason
there are very few women in the General Assembly (of which the
Moderator in 1947 was a woman).

In the Reformed Church of America and in the Evangelical and
Reformed Church the government of the local church rests in the
Consistory, composed of elders and deacons. The Consistory
(called in some Evangelical and Reformed Churches the Church
Council) takes responsibility, with the minister, for the spiritual
work of the church and also looks after the property and the
church charitable work. The Reformed Church of America does
not allow women to be members of consistories, and although
they have the right to vote, tradition still prevents it in many
churches. In the Evangelical and Reformed Church there has
been a gradual increase in the number of women in the consistories, some congregations have had them for as long as
twenty years, but most of the minority of churches which have
them at all have done so only recently, and very few women serve
on the higher boards of the Church.

The Churches of the Disciples of Christ closely resemble both
Congregational and Presbyterian Churches in church order.
Women are admitted as elders and deacons, but the report adds,
'The eldership is the point at which the strong tradition of sex
equality in the Disciple Churches breaks down. Only 1.1 per cent.
of Disciple Churches reported women elders—a total of five
women in three churches out of 277 reporting. This, however,
may be in excess of the proportion in the country as a whole. An
exceptionally well informed Disciples minister was surprised to
hear that there were any. The reason may probably be that the
elders administer the Lord's Supper: the minister does not
ordinarily do so'.

In the Methodist Churches of the United States women have
equal rights with men. About three-quarters of the Churches
reported that they had both men and women stewards. Stewards

correspond somewhat in function to congregational deacons, but are elected after nomination by the minister. The American report voices the complaint of some Methodist women that older women with means are usually chosen, and the younger, trained woman tends to be passed over. A Methodist Status of Women Commission has been working to get women to accept responsibility and Churches to appoint them as stewards. A higher proportion of local congregations appoint women to local boards in the Methodist than in any other Church. Class leaders, who played and still play in Great Britain so large a share in the development of Methodism as a Church, are not mentioned in the American report, though it is added that most Methodist Churches have 'a lay leader who takes a special responsibility with the minister for the spiritual welfare of the Church. Women are eligible but apparently only serve in smaller churches. At the Annual Conference level women have been lay leaders in extremely few cases'. The Evangelical United Brethren Churches have class leaders and a small number of Churches have women among them.

The position of women in the Protestant Episcopal Church of America differs markedly from their position in the Church of England. They serve on parish vestries if their diocesan convention decides that they may, and dioceses which permit them to serve appear to be in a minority. There are no examples of women serving as churchwardens, although in some dioceses they are allowed to do so. In 1946 the Episcopal General Convention had a woman delegate for the first time, but later two women were elected as lay representatives by their dioceses and by a majority vote the National Convention refused to allow them to be seated.

Lutheranism in America is divided into a number of Churches, some of them regional, others of them national according to the country of Europe from which their original founders came. The governing body of most Lutheran congregations is the Church Council. In most Lutheran Churches women are not allowed to serve on the Church Council (the governing body of the local church), but in the United Lutheran Church, the largest Lutheran group in the United States, they are allowed to serve unless the constitution of the local church forbids it. In Lutheran, as in Churches of the Congregational type, a meeting of all church members is held once a year, or failing that, such a meeting is summoned when a new minister is to be called or some important

decision has to be taken. Women are, as church members, eligible
to take part in these meetings and on the whole are taking a
growing share in them. It is interesting that one of the smaller
Churches, the Augustana Synod, has no women participating in
church government at the local level, but a fair proportion of
women are found on the regional and national boards of the
Church.

Most of the Churches which took part in the American survey
replied, in answer to a question, that they thought women were
playing a larger part in the affairs of the Churches now than they
were in 1940. The question was sent to local churches as well as to
denominational headquarters. Tradition against their participation is often far stronger than any legal barrier, and many women
reported that it is often enough for the minister to invite all men
to be present, or for the leading laymen to make it known that
they would not welcome the presence of women for women to
forego their legal rights in the interest of peace and harmony.
The custom in many churches of appointing officers for life
makes changes difficult. One new trend in the manner in which
the government of the local church is carried on is making for the
easy participation of women in places where they were before
excluded. In a number of denominations it is customary for local
churches to set up a church council or executive consisting of
representatives of the major organisations in the church. In some
denominations the function of such a body is advisory, but in
others it is a standing committee, responsible for executive decisions in the congregation, and the trustees of the property,
empowered to act for the local church, are appointed from this
body. Women are to be found with fair frequency among the
trustees of local churches of most denominations. The powers of
such a council vary from one local church to another. Women's
organisations are represented on the councils by women. The
American report draws an interesting comparison between the
position which women occupy in the Church and in civic life in
the United States. 'By and large, in church life women's participation in governing bodies is likely to begin with token representation
on national boards or committees. Gradually this is extended to
local church committees and then to local church boards. In civic
life women are most active at the lower rungs of the ladder.'

In South America, as has already been pointed out, the non-

Roman Churches are a small minority in the midst of a culture in which women have been poorly regarded and little educated. Most of the reports show that the leaders of the Churches, whether missionaries or not, do encourage women to take their share in the life of the Churches. The Methodist Church has in all countries opened church offices to women. In Chile women may become elders in the Presbyterian Church. The report from Venezuela speaks of the encouragement given to women to act in the Church by the Swedish missions. The whole picture may change when the women just now receiving an education from which their mothers were entirely debarred, emerge into the Church as fully participating members. In the meanwhile, the women's groups within many of the Churches help to train women to understand what the Church is and how it is governed and to accept responsibility. Where education is already more advanced, women are beginning to serve. Church women have played their part in the general upsurgence of women in the South American countries, expressed in the vigour with which they have worked for and obtained the vote.

South America is a stepping stone between those countries of the West in which the democratic principle is active in society, and the Church is as much pressed by social forces to take women into a share of its government as by any theological principle, and the Churches of Africa and the East where the Church itself pioneered in democratic practices before they made their appearance on the political scene. Here the Church has genuinely stood for a new conception of woman as a person in societies which accord her few or no legal rights or social privileges. For all such Churches there has had to be some kind of careful balance between not giving undue offence to social custom and making enough of a break with it to allow women to grow into responsible church-manship. By participating in the government of the churches, women (and men too for that matter) have learned what democracy means in actual practice, in the give and take between persons and sexes, in finding a common mind through differences and submitting opinions to the test of the mind of Christ. True, many Churches have failed in this; there are quarrels in churches about the possession of power, there are cliques and factions, there are sex and race discriminations. But all these failures are in the attempt at something difficult and splendid, and while a company of people still acknowledges the pattern of the mind of Christ and His lordship over the Church, there is always a standard dragging the community upwards.

It is everywhere true that social forces affect the participation of women in church government. There is no report from a Church in a Moslem land which gives any answer other than the word 'None' to questions about women's participation in church government. This is as true of ancient Churches like the Coptic as Churches founded by missionary endeavour in the past century. It is not, of course, true that missionaries to all foreign countries have found women in a markedly inferior status in society. In the Philippines the Protestant Churches, founded for the most part by American missionary endeavour, have women serving on all the church boards from local to national. The Japanese invasion drove the people into the hills and churches were destroyed. When the people returned it was often the women who took the lead in getting the Christian community together. The reason for this leadership and for their now long history of participation in church affairs is seen by the writers of the report as very largely due to the place women have occupied in the life of the community. 'It has been easy for men and women to work together because the Filipina has always had a place of recognition. She carried the purse and taught the children.' A Methodist Filipino bishop suggested: 'Filipinos have always considered women equal to men; at times they are looked upon as better for some types of leadership.' The Moderator of the United Evangelical Church. states: 'Men and women have always worked together as equals and sometimes women were given the place of greater honour. The law of the Philippines making the man the head of the house is imported and is of far later origin.'

There are not, however, many societies in which women have so favoured a position, though the report from Burma also says that much of the trade and shopkeeping in the country has been in the hands of women, that they have sound business instincts and have served the Church well in similar capacities. Elsewhere the story is often very different. 'Women's social position (and legal status) has always been very low, but it is now changing. It has always been better in the Church where the activity and ability of women have attracted attention' (Korea). This report goes on to show how the experience in managing affairs in the

M

Church was bringing Christian women very swiftly to the fore in the many social and political institutions which grew up after independence and flourished until the war mowed them down.

In China, Japan and Manchuria women take a full share in the life of the local Churches. Where there are women able to do so there seems to be little in the constitutions of the mission-planted Churches in these countries to prevent them from serving in the highest courts of the Churches. Christian missions from the earliest days worked to give girls as good an education as was given to boys, and the fruit of this is the presence in the Church of women trained not only in book-learning but in the democratic life of the Christian residential high school and college, the finest training for working with others in the Church. Many of the women of these countries who serve in positions of leadership in the Church are heads of educational institutions or hospitals and hold a high professional status. It is a notable comparison that although in the West there are far more women in positions of influence and responsibility in society, a far smaller proportion of them seem to have time to give to their Church than in the East. The reason for this must be further discussed. It is also true that, compared to the woman who shares in church government at the highest level in the West, her counterpart in the East is far more experienced and educated ecuminically. Few women in the West have travelled so widely or know so much about Churches of other denominations as some of the oriental women leaders. Sometimes the missions, but much more often the World's Y.W.C.A., have been responsible for the superb education of these women.

The result of Japanese occupation was to set back the participation of women in the work of the Churches. In Manchuria this was particularly noticeable. Here women were forbidden to serve on boards and committees, and as the education of girls was severely restricted there are not now the younger educated women who ought to be stepping into these places. The Chinese report points out that Christian women tend to take the lead in local communities partly because they are better educated, but also because they have learned the wise exercise of leadership in the Church, but there are not enough women to fill all the places of leadership that are open for the right woman to take. The report from Japan remarks that there seem to be fewer psychological barriers to the sharing of leadership between men and women in countries of the East than in those of the West. 'Lack of social experience and unequal educational background would seem to be the more simple and practical explanation for unequal participation. Under the new constitution women are to have equal educational and political opportunities which eventually will result in better preparation for the rank and file of women to share more fully in church life.'

'Where Churches are working under an old constitution,' says the report from India, 'there is little official recognition of the place of women in the administration of the Church. This is not always a hardship, however, as actual practice may be considerably more liberal than the rules would indicate. There may be variations between different missions of the same denomination.' An example is given of one Baptist Church still working under a manual entered according to the Act of Congress in 1853, while another Baptist Church which re-wrote its constitution in 1946 accords equal rights to women in explicit terms. Such a constitution does something to hand on to the Church in written form the position which single women missionaries had acquired by virtue of their work. Too often it was supposed that they were accorded status in the Church because they were missionaries and not because they were women, and church bodies have been reluctant to accord the same status to women other than missionaries. The effect of this was to cause women missionaries and those working with them to be reluctant to have their piece of work pass into the hands of the Church, and mission control was therefore maintained longer than it should have been because it seemed the only way of keeping that work from passing virtually into the hands of male supervisors in the Church.

There is one point at which in India and in other countries also the help of women is genuinely sought by the church leaders. In these countries moral discipline is an important part of the Church's function if it is to maintain Christian moral standards in non-Christian society. Among the Bhil Christians in Central India who are simple animists and babes in the faith, the United Church of North India encourages the election of women elders by the congregations. It is quite common for there to be an equal number of men and women elders. These women share in the disciplinary functions of the elders and also assist in the handling of the elements at the Holy Communion. The Church of India, Burma and Ceylon (Anglican) has also adopted an office of women elders. A woman is elected by the women of the Church and is then dedicated to the task by the minister before the whole congregation. Her task is to assist in all cases of the discipline of women and girls, to raise the moral standards of Christian women, to be responsible for order and discipline in public worship and to encourage Christian giving. She may perhaps be an illiterate village woman: the one qualification is that she should have the respect of the women of the congregation. 'It is becoming fairly widespread in the Churches,' says the report, 'that women should be associated with men in all cases of discipline where women are involved, e.g. adultery. There have been tragic cases in the past of women being accused, tried and sentenced by men in church courts without a woman's advice being sought.'

In Africa, too, even in very young and simple Churches women are beginning to undertake similar functions. A report from the Cameroons describes the election of a woman elder in a Church which had been established for fifty years entirely under the leadership of men. 'There was no disturbance as the pastor called the woman to the front. Nobody made any undue remarks or unkind noises as she stood solemnly and awkwardly before them. They voted. There were one dozen brave warriors against, but two hundred in favour. Before a congregation elects an elder the Session recommends the nominee. In the Session it was one of the pastors who suggested her name. Of eighteen elders twelve were in favour and six against. "Women are not ready for such leadership." . . . The few women elders may be said to serve helpfully in judging cases of women and girls' discipline. On other topics they seldom speak much. The presence of a woman on the session helps to reassure women and girls when they are called to appear before that august body.' From another part of Africa comes a description of a woman elder at the Communion Service passing the elements to the congregation. Strapped to her back are the twin babies which, if she were not a Christian, would have been left in the bush to die of exposure. The participation of women in church life may seem little enough but as a report from Eastern Nigeria points out, 'Rarely in village life do men and women meet together for discussion. They have their separate meetings.

Consequently women are shy and loth to express an opinion in some of the meetings in which they are representatives'. One report describes a meeting for women in a remote village. A few men were present at the back, in the capacity of watchdogs to see what the women were doing. Discussion was invited, but nobody spoke. Presently in the silence a grunt was heard from the back of the room and immediately the signal was given a lively discussion broke out among the women. In Churches which are not Presbyterian in church order there are women charged with spiritual and moral oversight. In certain Congregational Churches they are spoken of as the senior women. These women wear a uniform and meet weekly for consultation. Many of them are also deacons in the congregations.

The great cry from Africa is the need for the training of women, not only because they are illiterate and totally unused to assuming responsibility in any community, but because the slick and shallow freedom of the western world is being brought by the film, press and radio, and a narrow and embittered nationalism is demanding that Africans shall have all the outward trappings of European and American 'civilisation'. The old custom of separation of the sexes in church services is changing in many parts of West Africa, but, says one of the reports, 'The man with the older wife, or the poorly dressed wife will not be seen sitting with his family. It is the man with the smartly dressed young wife, wanting to show her off, who will break with custom. It is a social pressure'. The younger women are not able to distinguish the good from the tawdry in all that comes to Africa from the West, and the criteria of a judgment can only be given by education and training in the best. There is feverish haste at present to train leaders for Africa's independence, and no doubt leaders in the political, administrative and academic sphere will be men. But that will not touch the deep springs of the life of the people which flow from mother to child through the endless customs and traditions of the home: only the training of women can do that.

It seems true to say that in nearly all Churches the world over women are taking a steadily increasing responsibility in the management of the affairs of the Churches at the local and the national level. War increased the need for women to take the place of men who went away, and many Churches have learned to value the service of women in a new way. As has been pointed out already, whether women make an effective contribution or not depends more on the atmosphere in a Church than on the legal position, although of course legal barriers can prevent some forms of service. The women who wrote the reports are frank about women's failures. Few of them know or apply themselves to learning committee procedure or to read a balance sheet: on the other hand, they have a lot of experience in managing on small budgets (the women are the spenders of the family income the world over), and sometimes their advice is shrewd but too homely for the business sense of it to be seen by men who bring to the affairs of the Church the techniques of business. Women are nearly always at a disadvantage, they say, when there is only one of them on a committee, especially if women have not served before. There is far too easy a way for men to say that 'they had a woman once and she was no good—talked too much or not to the point', and thus dismiss a whole sex. Many of the reports, especially that from the United States, include remarks from ministers on their experiences with women committee members. A number say that women talk less than the men because they limit themselves to the few subjects of which they have personal knowledge. They remark that a woman has more patience with detail, thinks more in terms of the effects of certain actions on persons and yet is often prepared to be much more outspoken in order to deal with a difficult personal situation, while a group of men will quite often temporise—dealing with the church caretaker is given as an example of this. There seems to be little resentment, though there is a tinge of it where the vexed question of the spending of money raised by women groups being spent by all-male committees comes up. Another subject on which women feel rather strongly is when the membership of the central governing committee in the church is kept all-male, not because of theological scruples, but because men enjoy the atmosphere of a men's club: they point out that the Church is not a club but a community of men and women, that each sex has a unique and irreplaceable contribution to make to the whole and that the life of the Church is the poorer if the effort of enabling each to contribute is not made. That it *is* an effort in understanding is freely admitted, nor is it only men who are unwilling to make the effort. There are many women who prefer to work in all-women's groups, and some even go so far as to set themselves to show minister and church lay leaders just how much more efficient the women's group is than the governing group in the Church!

Perhaps it is not always realised that the acceptance of responsibility as an elected member of a congregation is a very new thing for women. When George Fox at the end of the seventeenth century made it quite clear that in the Society of Friends there should be no difference between men and women in directing the affairs of the Society and speaking in meetings, he found that in fact women would not speak. He therefore started separate women's groups and in his letters commanded the men to see to it that women Friends belonged to them. Here questions of behaviour and discipline, as they affected women and girls, were discussed. At the same time women were encouraged to share in the general meetings, and in the eighteenth century the separate meetings for women Friends were abolished and they fully shared with the others. All the difficulties voiced today about women unused to responsibility taking part in general meetings are to be found in the comments and disagreements of the Friends.

It is nonsense to say that women have never had any power in the Churches: they have had immense power, but power in the form of influence, which is irresponsible power. Nobody can call to account the wife or mother who gets her way with husband or son and is known to be the real director of his opinion and vote. This is the form of power to which women, especially very able women, have been confined by their exclusion from responsible power. Wherever democratic ideals prevail in society, influence of all kinds is discredited. Open attempts are made to prevent pressure on political leaders and on those who make appointments, issue honours and privileges and make executive decisions in every walk of life. That influence is discredited is not to say that it is abolished. Women have wielded influence with very great skill over the centuries and many still prefer it to any form of responsibility which brings them out into the open. But the choice between influence and responsibility is one that women have to make, and Churches have to make in relation to women.

VI

CHANGE AND OPPORTUNITY

I T IS EXPECTED of last chapters that they shall draw some
conclusions and, in the case of a book which has described the
growth of certain present-day institutions, that there should be
some word about a possible future. On a world scale such tasks
are too intimidating to be embarked upon, and it would be easier
by far to leave the picture of the life and work of women in the
Church just as it stands. There is one reason why this cannot be
done. The reports on which this book is based contain not only
facts, but reflection on the facts by those who wrote them and
their associates in the collecting of material. Reflection is therefore
as proper to this book as statement. It often appears in a report
that the arrival of the World Council enquiry gave those who were
deeply engaged in women's work in the Churches the opportunity
to sit back for a moment and ask themselves and others what they
thought all the work was for, whether they were satisfied with it
and especially where they placed it in the total life of the Church
and of society.

There are perhaps two main questions which are implicit in the
comments made in the reports. The first is the question whether at
this moment in the history of a distracted world the Churches are
really making the fullest uses of all their resources of personnel in
order to fulfil their mission in the world. Are the gifts and willingness of women being used to the best advantage by the Churches?
This book is an attempt to answer that question. By showing
what women have done in places where they have been given, or
have created, opportunity, it may suggest ways in which the
service of women could be enlarged, the life of the Church
enriched and its message strengthened. There is no other answer
than 'Look and judge'.

Behind this question lies another, far more difficult to define, let alone to answer. It can perhaps be put partially in this way. Are women, married or not, being helped by the Church to understand the problems of the age as they affect women, to play their part in modern life as Christians and as women? But this question cannot be answered unless there is an understanding of what women are, and what their place in society is. What is needed is that there should start within the Churches, among those who care about this matter, a process of thought about women in modern society, an imaginative act of understanding, and entering into, a total experience. For there has been a revolutionary change in the place of women in society. Women not only live a very different life from that of their grandparents, but—and this is even more important—they think differently about themselves. It has been left on the whole to secular thinkers and writers to try to understand this revolution and such books as *Male and Female* by Margaret Mead, who writes as an anthropologist, and *Le deuxième Sexe* by the French existentialist philosopher, Simone de Beauvoir, are eagerly read because they seek to enter into the total experience of women in the modern world and to provide some signposts in a bewildering scene. But Christian writers are silent except for the quantities of practical little books, many of them valuable within their limited range on Christian marriage and Christian home life. Except for Professor Karl Barth's exegesis of the creation story in the third volume of his *Dogmatik*, there is nothing to put beside the books here mentioned.

The reason for this lack of prophetic imaginative writing from the Christian side is at least in part that the Churches are deeply divided in what they think about the place of women in the modern world and in the Church. The woman who accepts the judgment of men on most subjects, who is happy in the small practical tasks to be found in every congregation and seeks protection from the harsh problems of the modern world, will certainly find a niche for herself in the Church and feel that she belongs. And it is quite right that she should do so. Thousands of women the world over expect the Church to be a place where, free for a short period from the continuous demands of families which look to them for everything, they can find rest and refreshment for the soul, friendship and a simple outlet for their desire to help others. One of the reports summarises the activities of women in many congregations in the following words. 'Serving meals at religious gatherings and social functions, raising money by bazaars and fêtes and devices of all kinds; touring as choirs, concert parties, entertainments and competitions; individual church women hold house functions and afternoon parties, musical luncheons, childern's concerts, puppet shows, etc. In many Churches women prepare the Sacramental bread and wine for the communion service.' To get the picture quite right one must add that this report also describes other activities, such as organising the Women's World Day of Prayer and work for the United Nations Association. But none the less, it is true that in a great many Churches women work at projects of the kind quoted with immense energy and organising power but with decreasing conviction, at least among some. 'We rather wonder whether the endless cups of tea which women do and are expected to prepare are the only or even the chief contribution which women have to make to the Church.' Here speaks another voice, the voice of the woman who is not caught into the busy round of the life of a vigorous congregation with more than half her self. Beyond her is the woman who simply cannot imagine herself ever being able, whatever her goodwill, to throw herself into the kind of social life which is the *sine qua non* of so many successful congregations. 'If women take an active part in the life and work of the Church it very often demands so much time that they have no energy left for friendships and family relationships,' says one report. There are large numbers of women who are Christians and members of their Churches, but their share in the life of the Church is limited by their feeling that their main work for Christ lies outside the actual walls of the church in society where they work. Often they feel that their situation is not understood in the Church and they do not get from it the spiritual nourishment which they know themselves to need. They also mark the contrast between the workaday world in which, in very many walks of life, it is true, as one report puts it, that 'contributions are judged on their merits and not by whether they come from a man or a woman', and the Church where this is often not the case, where 'women are seldom stimulated to use their varied gifts' and where 'it is doubtful whether the variety of their gifts is recognised'. The woman of an independent cast of mind who has earned her own living and perhaps that of dependents and is accustomed to taking her share in decisions without diffidence usually finds it difficult to be at home in the church.

Unfortunately, the very large number of older women in the Churches have succeeded to an extraordinary degree in creating the impression that they are *the real woman*, the home-loving type, liking the social life of the Church, content to let the men settle all questions of policy and action. They find it difficult to believe that 'the modern woman' can be a Christian type of womanhood. 'Ministers and congregations,' says one report, 'are hidebound by tradition. Leading circles in the Church are disposed to be conservative, their view of society is *patriarchal* and their inclination towards the old ways affects their view of the place of women in society and therefore in the Church. . . . The patriarchal conception of the relation of men and women is even stronger in parsonages than it is among the people generally.' Other writers would not put it as strongly as this, and some would not have cause to do so, but in nearly every Church it remains true that there is an underlying fear of the modern woman, of her independence of character, her acceptance of herself as a person in herself and not merely for man. It is not much use for the Church to tell this type of woman that the rôle of woman is that of help-meet to man, that it is an honourable rôle and that man cannot be complete without her. This does not really mean anything to the woman who is the child of her age unless she is first assured that the Church accepts her own discovery of herself as fully a person. She is no longer happy to be the agent of man's self-fulfilment, but neither is she able to accept the heady individualism of the pioneers of the women's movement to whom so often men were at best a necessary evil in a female paradise, and a woman who married was lost to the cause. She is not afraid of her womanhood, not afraid even to seek the dependence that lies within the outer shell of the independence with which she faces the world in which she has to earn her living and make the grade in a society shaped by man. She wants to put all her powers into the task of home-making and family rearing which have absorbed most women all down the ages.

But at this point perhaps it would be wise to turn away for a moment from the division of mind within the Churches (and it is not a division on sex lines) about what woman ought to be and do in order to be the type of a Christian woman in the mid-twentieth century, to something on which all are agreed, and begin there. Women make a unique contribution in the Church through their work in bearing children and nurturing them in the faith. It is admirably portrayed in the report from Syria, in which a member of the Armenian Church, surely the most persecuted and the most tenacious Church in all Christian history, describes what she calls 'the main contribution of women to our Church'. 'Almost every believer in our Church has his or her mother as the source for Christian faith and conduct. All this is done in an unassuming quietness, they deeming it beyond the limits of modesty to speak about it, but witnessing through a Christian life even in times of great suffering and persecution. It is the story of my own mother, and I am sure thousands of others, that in the days of fear and disaster at the time of the First World War, confined to a stable in hiding, she drew her strength through her only companion besides her children, the Bible and her daily reading from it, and she did not hesitate, even at the risk of her life, to go out at dusk when the streets would be quiet and utter a prayer inside the walls of a ruined church. Children who have witnessed this cannot lose their faith for they have grasped the meaning of Christian faith.' In this description all will agree that the type of the Christian woman is fully displayed.

What more important work could a woman possibly do in the Church or in society than this? Why should any woman with the opportunity of marriage and a family seek any wider sphere, or any woman without a family doubt that the crown of life has been withheld from her? This is woman's work, her life and her fulfilment. To many in the Churches it is beyond imagining why women should show any interest in anything else, and the modern woman's restlessness is attributed to her unwillingness to accept without qualification such a rôle. But the woman writing from Syria continues her account thus—'Things have changed since the first war when the Armenians, dispersed to all parts of the world, became subject to various influences, mostly leading away from home and Church.' The Burmese report makes the same comment on what the upheavals of society have done to young people. 'War is essentially lawless and morally disintegrating in its effects. With most schools closed for four or five years children and young people were at a loose end. The roving groups of bandits which now terrorise Burma are one evidence of the lasting

effects of this disintegration. The wildness and restlessness of
youth, in a country in which formerly a deep respect for elders
was a leading virtue, is another. In Christian homes and communities women feel the burden of this problem.' The two writers
clearly see that the work of the Christian home can be destroyed
by society. The Armenians and the Karens—and many others—
have seen the catastrophic sweeping away of old sanctions and
standards. In countries where they are eroded away by slower,
less spectacular but equally effective means, women are slower to
realise the implications. The English report puts it forcibly in this
way: 'Besides a great deal of kindly sentimental talk about the
woman in the home, it should be brought home to Christian
women that the majority of husbands, sons and brothers have
given up religious observance. It is difficult for the home to
compete with the influence of the school: the Church functions
somewhat feebly in a secularised society, and Christian women
have not sought, nor have they been stimulated to seek, better
and more practical training. It is probable that a great number of
women have not troubled to notice this, to think about it, ask
advice or even discuss it with their children. It has gone by
default largely because of our dependence on inheritance rather
than on active Christianity.'

'Had a jolly breakfast,' a young man of 13, pupil at one of
England's greatest schools, wrote in his diary in 1905, 'talked to
Mother about the kind of things she can understand.' Mother
indeed could be happily engaged in the pursuit of dress, female
philanthropy or whatever was her own preoccupation, sure in the
knowledge (if she gave it a thought) that the young man would
receive from school and university the fruits of the Christian
cultural tradition of centuries old growth in Western Europe, and
that he would then pass to work beside his father in the family
profession or the service of his country, still safely within the
same tradition. Nor was the security of a continuing tradition
the prerogative of the rich alone: for the poor also the sanctions
of the home were supported by those of the local community
where the young person was known and his behaviour commented upon. Even in the vastness of America the social group
kept fairly tight hold on the young and there were moral standards
which could hardly be broken unwittingly. All Western nations
had their own outcastes, the criminal and so-called ineducable,

the nameless and destitute of the great cities with whom the respectable rich and the respectable poor had equally little to do. Outside the Western tradition the same unity of purpose between the home and the larger society in which it was set prevailed also: there was no radical break in the purpose of the African home and the tribe, of the Hindu home and the caste. Education, begun in the home through the nurture of the mother, continued as the father introduced the child to the wider culture of the village and taught the boy his own skills. There was no need for the mother to go out of her home to know fully what the culture of her people was or to learn how to equip her child for participation in it.

The home has never stood alone as the educator of the young: there has always been the larger family encasing and reinforcing the culture of the home, including the grandparents and the more distant relations and also the dead of past generations represented often in the objects they made in and around the home, who are a part of the family tradition in which the child is nurtured. Outside this larger family is the village or township, the working associates of the father, the servants or the masters closely bound to the family's life. All these buttress and support the parents in any deeply-rooted society and assist in education. The educative function of the society is given religious sanctions; it is the priests who preserve and amplify the tradition, who deal with breaches and who shape the patterns of myth and symbol, ceremony and sacrifice, which, with their powerful hold on the imagination, govern relationships between the sexes, between men and the soil and between the social groups in the larger whole. The Church brought new elements into this universal pattern of stable localised societies: it did not provide a religious sanction for the way of life of one tribe or nation, it was a genuinely universal society cradled within other societies and transforming the natural life of man by giving him a second centre of attachment. The Church was different from the temple, Jewish, Hindu or any other, in being a community first and foremost and only secondly and subsequently a localised place of religious observance. In Western Europe the Church gathered into itself many of the remaining customs of paganism, giving them a Christian tinge: gradually, as the older cultures of tribes and Roman city alike fell into decay, the Church itself became almost synonymous with society.

It was from this identification on its corrupting side that the Reformers tried to free the Church, but while they did that other forces grew up to take society in charge, forces only now reaching their full strength.

Where do we now stand? We live in what is generally known as 'a mixed society', and all societies except those of the most remote and inaccessible tribes are mixed societies, though the strength of the different ingredients varies. Old communities based on the land and held together by religious custom receive into their midst the products of the new forces of science and technology: everywhere the old is disrupted by the new, the young move off to mines and cities beyond the control alike of home and community. Escape from the sanctions of the group into the anonymous individualism of the mass becomes a possible, and to many a very welcome, alternative to the life of the group. For the more able and intelligent, who can hope to take their share in the development of science and technology, a new and exhilarating form of power is opened up to their grasp: there seems to be no limit to what man can do, and gods and natural calamities alike lose their power to inspire awe beside the mighty works of man.

Scientific and technological culture are the work of the intellect and manual skill of man, that is to say, of the male sex. The contribution of women to this process has been very small indeed. Yet the traditional life of woman has been profoundly changed by it, perhaps more profoundly than that of the man. For the two-faced aspect which this new power wears, its beneficence and its destruction are clear to the woman in her own intimate personal life. In most primitive societies, and not a few more sophisticated ones, man may expose himself to danger and glory, but it is woman who bears the unalleviated loads, on whom the residual tasks fall, which no one else can be bribed or compelled to perform. Even in societies where she has been rather more highly valued the best years of her life have been given to the bearing of children only to see a fair proportion of them die in infancy or childhood from famine or disease or congenital defects. The whole aspect of a woman's life is changed by the knowledge that she need not bear a dozen children in order that two or three may reach maturity, and that she has it in her power to prevent much suffering and many handicaps. No woman who understands what science has done to prevent and control disease and dispel ignorance is going lightly to call it evil. On the other hand, it is for the most part hidden from her that the restlessness she feels in her home comes from the same source. The advent of the technical society has made the life of the home infinitely less varied and satisfying. Husbands go out to work. There is a wealth of meaning in the phrase: their work is no longer in or near the home where the woman shared in it or at least knew what was going on. The work of modern society is for the greater part concentrated in factories and offices, in institutions, such as hospitals, laboratories, in vast undertakings such as railways, engineering and building projects. Of its very essence modern work has to be thus concentrated, because it is a co-operative undertaking not of the family but of the working unit. Nor can children be prepared to work in such a society except in the school, and at an early age in the specialised school some distance from home. Home is no longer either an educating or a working unit. She is free of some of the claims and demands which tied her forebears—but the price is loneliness, a feeling that she does not share either her husband's or her children's life and yet has no special niche of her own in society. It is as though the main stream of the life of society no longer passes through the home: the stream has shifted and the home, with the woman in it, is left high and dry on the bank; she longs for her place in the working world and because of her children she is concerned to be a part and not a mere spectator of the social processes which, with the home, shape their lives.

All these factors, and still more the tendency of taxation to go on rising steadily, coupled with the raising of the age at which children may leave school and become wage-earners, turn the woman's mind towards work outside her home for at least part of the day. One of the main changes in the labour situation in Europe and America, shown by figures published since the war, is the increased number of women in employment. The figures are not quite so high as they were in the middle of the war, but they are far higher than they were before the war. According to the United States Census Bureau seventeen million women were employed in 1947, just on a third of all American women. The 1948 figures showed that of employed women 38 per cent. were single, 46 per cent. married, 16 per cent. widowed or divorced; of 451 types of work listed, 442 were open to women: a million women owned their own businesses and 173,000 managed their own farms. Why do these women work? Because they have to. In a post-war study of women workers in an industrial community, 9 out of 10 women supported themselves and over half were also supporting others. All the single women, all the widowed and divorced and 84 per cent. of the married women gave the need of support for themselves and others as the reason for working. Sixteen per cent. of the women were the *sole* wage-earners in family groups of *four or more* persons. Other similar surveys have given similar results. Women with children under school age numbered 800,000 in a total of 4 million working mothers, and nearly all were widowed or divorced or had husbands who did not earn. In spite of the clear indication that women work to support themselves and others, women's wages are low. The average wage for all workers was $57.54 a week, for unskilled men $49.79, and for women, skilled and unskilled, $41.39.

In Great Britain the picture is remarkably similar. Thirty per cent.[1] of women between 15 and 60 are at work. They constitute a third of the total labour force. Fifty per cent. are single, 40 per cent. are married and 10 per cent. are widows (fairly high widows' pensions paid by the State with restriction on employment may account for this difference). In textiles and the clothing industry they form 58 and 67 per cent. of the total labour force. This is a close parallel to the United States and shows how women have followed what used to be their work in the home into the factories to which machines have drawn it. They have a big share in the distributive trades, 41 per cent., and in catering. In Germany, owing to heavy war losses the numbers of women working to support families have greatly increased. Nevertheless the disparity of income between men and women workers is large and strict control of employment gives priority to men with families. The problem of women working who have small children has exercised the Churches in Germany and they have also turned their attention to the particular problem of the very large number of women for whom the chances of marriage are infinitesimal because of the large losses of men in the war. In the Eastern zone the employment of married women and the placing of children in state nurseries has been enforced by compulsion.

[1] Counting part-time work and paid domestic work for an employer, the figure is 43.8 per cent.

N

Industrialisation and the cultivation of estates for cash crops have enormously increased the number of women in economic employment in Eastern countries. Women workers in India, for example, numbered over 48 million according to the 1931 census. This figure was a third of the total working population of the country. Writing of this, an Indian contributor to the survey says, 'It is widely believed that while man contributes directly to the social economy woman does so only indirectly through the domestic economy. But it is doubtful whether in the history of any community the production and distribution of wealth have depended wholly on the contribution of its male members. Women have always shared in agriculture and gardening, and in ancient India women were employed in many economic schemes and attention was given to the conditions of female employment.' The greatest proportion of these 48 million work in agriculture, but there were over a million women in organised industries, i.e. working for an employer. Of these about a quarter were in factories and a far larger number worked on plantations. Women were excluded from underground work in the coal mines in India after 1937, but 10,000 were taken back in the middle of the war. Women do heavy work in road-making and mending, building and other public works. 'Why do our Indian women work?' asks one of the correspondents. 'The low wages of men drive women to work. Many of our women workers are those whose families are indigent, who are widows or deserted women without means. Most of our women workers are illiterate, ignorant and unskilled, too weak to better their own lot. Their wages are universally lower than those of men, even for the same work. Another discouraging factor is that women who work are liable to lose their social status. This is due in part to the old superstition that extra domiciliary work is unworthy of a woman, and in part to the widespread belief that the woman who is exposed to outside contacts cannot be chaste. These views are utterly wrong and are gradually giving place to a more modern outlook. As long as social stigma and suspicion continue the ordinary working woman cannot but have a sense of inferiority.' Since the war women have taken up new forms of work in India as in other countries, but one of the most striking changes has been the large increase in the number of women from middle-class homes seeking employment. The father who used to think it a matter of honour to support his daughters, provide them with a dowry and a husband, now perhaps has lost all in the troubles following partition, or if he has not, he often wonders whether it is, in these days, the best service to his daughter to marry her off without a training or the experience of work, to which she might return if calamity overtook her. In India the work that the nineteenth century reformers did still needs to be done—to make sure that no woman is compelled to work because the wages of men are so low as to make it impossible to support a family, and to remove women from work such as underground work in mines, heavy work on the roads, which endanger their health and that of their children. But women have come to stay in the economic life of India, and many Indian women are labouring with all their power to obtain the legislation and the inspection for its enforcement which would improve the working conditions of Indian women, and to raise as many as possible above the level of the unskilled. Working women are themselves taking their position more seriously, and in 1945, 26,000 women were members of trade unions.

These few facts and figures are necessarily scrappy and incomplete. They are only meant to be enough to show that economic employment is a major factor in the lives of women the world over. Even the African woman in her village now takes her eggs and the produce of her garden to market and has a little money of her own, while in an increasing number of countries a very large range of employment is open to women on terms which, since the war, have approximated more closely to those of men. The purpose of sketching even in so brief a fashion these facts which portray that woman in the modern world is an economic worker, is to ask the question whether the Churches have as yet laid this to heart and grasped its full implications. For the fact is not just that about a third of the women of many countries are in economic employment, but that wherever this is so the great majority of women have had the experience of working and many have skills not at the moment in use. There are many in the Churches whose view is that a woman should not work, that something must have gone badly wrong with the normal and right position of women in society if they have to. The motive behind this thinking, particularly among men, is often protective, but too often it stops short at the sentiment of protection and therefore becomes sentimentality. The ideal, it is felt, would be a return to the economic dependence of women on fathers and husbands, but no one seriously believes that such a thing is possible, or works to achieve it. Yet the feeling that women do not really *belong* in the economic sphere, that their presence there is at best an unfortunate necessity, prevents many Christians from understanding the new problems and opportunities before women. Such matters as the United Nations Commission on the status of women; the work done by the International Labour Office on the opinions of Governments on equal pay for men and women; the examination by Unesco of educational opportunities for women and girls— these receive little or no comment from Church leaders, nor do there seem to be groups of Christian women giving any enthusiastic support to the efforts of women's movements, governments and the United Nations Organisation to raise the status of women in countries where it is low, and to extend to the woman as worker the freedom which in so many countries she has gained as citizen.

The general neglect by Christians to give thought to the present place of woman in society, more especially as worker, arises from a number of different causes. The Churches uphold and support the Christian ideal of marriage as the life-long union of one man with one woman, and in times such as the present, when that standard is being lowered in society, they are opposed in principle to any social change which might seem to lead to easier divorce. Because they have happened at the same time, it is very easy to put the economic independence of women and the rising tide of divorce into the relation of cause and effect. It is perfectly true that women who have been divorced are able to support themselves by their own work, but that is not the same as proving that the possibility of employment puts divorce into women's minds. The increasing economic employment of women is one of those things which may have many results, good and bad: granted that perhaps a few women are able to leave their husbands because they will not thereby become absolutely destitute, is it not also to be argued that the employment of women has led to women sharing a burden which used to fall exclusively on men—the support of old parents? Indeed, the immense increase in the proportion of old people in modern society would constitute an intolerable burden on the shoulders of young fathers of families were they not assisted by the earnings of their sisters and in some cases of their wives. Again, the Churches are deeply concerned about the family, and rightly stress, with the psychologists to back them up, the importance to the child of its mother's care in the first years of its life. An argument constantly heard is that married women go out to work and neglect their children. Those who deal with labour questions, on the other hand, say that women with small children form a very small proportion of the total of women working, that those who seek work stipulate that they want part-time work near home and at hours which they can manage: surveys show that of the comparatively small numbers of working women with little children the very great majority work because of economic need, many have been widowed or deserted, some work temporarily to clear a debt, or make a vital purchase, others have husbands out of work or sick. Some, nervous victims of the war, work because work is a narcotic—one wonders where they would be if they did not work—some out of selfish motives of wanting more money and less home responsibility (and perhaps these too with their hidden disorders of personality need more sympathy than blame).

In itself the economic employment of women is neither good nor bad, but can be made either. The most important thing about it is simply that it IS, that it is a part of modern life. It is the way by which the modern woman tries to find her way back into the working society where she always had her place until the mid-nineteenth century, unless she belonged to the few rich. It is her means of finding her place in the community beyond the home, which takes her children from an early age. Many women who used to engage in voluntary service outside the home as their means of self-expression are now employed. Once Christians fully accept the fact of women working, they can begin to help shape the conditions.

Such an acceptance of the fact that woman is a worker would cause a very big change in the treatment of women in the Churches. The Churches are most successful with married women, especially older married women: they hardly touch that 30 per cent. of women who are economically employed, and this 30 per cent. contains a high proportion of women in the prime of life and a significant proportion of women who are more than unskilled labour—skilled responsible workers and potential leaders. Basically women are kept out of certain offices in the Church, and operate mainly in groups with other women, because a certain picture of what a woman is prevails in many church circles. Though few would admit as much, many Christians believe that the woman is a secondary being, an agent enabling and completing man: probing will uncover the existence of ancient taboos about women's impurity, still lurking in most unexpected places. Many of the women who have written in the reports quoted in this book feel a sense of despair about the way in which Bible texts are used to justify and support already held opinions about the place of women in the Church. When Churches are in a desperate position for lack of man-power, all sorts of service is gladly accepted from women: when the situation is eased, theological reasons against women doing this kind of work are at once raised. Some women feel quite as strongly the debasement of theology involved in this procedure as true injustice to women! Other reports speak of gifted women who have gained qualifications in divinity, for whom the Church finds no place. Very many reports refer to the low pay and status accorded to full time women workers in the Church and to the uncertainty which surrounds their position. There is something of a vicious circle in regard to this: many able women do not enter the direct service of the Church because they know that they will find themselves committed to what one report describes as 'a collection of good works' or even to all the odd jobs in a congregation, some of them doubtfully valuable, many of them easily performed by those without training. Therefore among those offering to serve in the Church there are, if the truth be told, a fair sprinkling who are not capable of carrying larger responsibility than is at present given to them, and they supply in some Churches an excuse for not enlarging the sphere of service for women.

If there is one thing more than another that these reports show quite clearly it is the uselessness of theoretical argument about what women can, may or ought to do. Such arguments quickly lead into the quagmire of discussing what woman is, as though she were a given and finalised collection of attributes and limitations. As Simone de Beauvoir points out in the book already cited, man is a continuous becoming, constantly exhibiting new and surprising powers of controlling and indeed creating his environment; and the same is true of woman, that she is not a biologically determined creature, so that one can say what she is because one knows what she has been in the past, when she has had to relate herself to particular social conditions and to live within the sphere that man allowed her. She, like man, is a creature with unrealised resources, and she is far behind man in this historical process of showing what she is, because of centuries in which her life was dominated by the necessity of preserving the race. Therefore, says Simone de Beauvoir, she must 'display her possibilities', not stand and argue. Karl Barth has said something much the same, that in this question of women in the Church it is for women to 'show what they can do'.

This act of 'showing what she can do' must not be regarded as a piece of display, or as intended to show men or other women that women are capable and ought to be given a larger share in the work of the Church than they have in some places. It is not in order to prove something to others, but as a matter of her own integrity that the woman who feels that she has God-given powers must prove them by exercising them. Society, the community outside the institutional Church (which is just as much the world for which Christ died as the Church is), lies open before her, and if she fulfills her calling by using her gifts there and obeys God in so doing, she *is* serving the Church. More than that, she is serving the Church in a way it particularly needs and a way that women especially have it in their power to serve. Many of the reports show anxiety about the way in which the Church in many places is cut off from the life of society. It appears to many outside the Church, even those who wish to be inside, to be a group concerned with its own affairs, expressing its desire for those who are outside to come in, but finding newcomers to the faith difficult to assimilate unless they will conform to the routine life of those already within the walls of the church. Some of the Indian correspondents speak with considerable anxiety about the fact that because the first Christians had to make a radical break with society which was Hindu or Moslem in all social actions, now the Church finds itself out of the main stream of the nation's life and cut off from India's cultural heritage. In the West a similar separation is felt: the Church, which used to be the larger community at worship, is now a group within a disintegrated community. Many of the services which used to be rendered by the Churches to society, effecting an easy and natural link between the Church and the larger community, are now performed by the State or the city or town, or by voluntary organisations subsidised by public funds. The Church has so far succeeded in its historic mission that it has taught society to be merciful to the weak, and care for the aged and the orphaned. Many of the women who look at the Church and decide that its direct service is not the place for them find their way into the new social services. One of the greatest achievements of women since their emancipation a hundred years ago is the creation of new professions which are now indispensable to society, the professions of highly skilled and trained social workers. But social work, which began as the expression of Christian love can easily degenerate into mere efficiency: care for the sick, poor, aged and helpless can be just a concern with the tidiness of society, with not wasting lives and time through disease, malnutrition, illiteracy, social incompetence and so on. Immense, because very subtle, powers pass into the hands of the modern State through the possession of an instrument, commonly known as welfare, affecting the lives of citizens so closely that it gives the State a wealth of knowledge about everyone, together with the power to use that knowledge. The welfare State operates almost entirely through the services of women, who make up the bulk of the social workers, all the nurses, and a large proportion of the teachers. Christians amongst these workers are to be found in large numbers because of the strong appeal these vocations make to the Christian desire to help one's fellow men, but to keep the ideal of Christian love from degenerating into an efficiency concerned with techniques rather than persons is a very difficult task. Many women engaged in welfare work of all kinds find themselves exercising a pastoral ministry, a ministry which the Church does not yet recognise or assist the woman to fulfil. Her long experience as the homemaker, the one who brings forth and cares for young life, makes the woman the one of the human partnership most capable of turning into something of a home for humanity the society which man has created and de-personalised by his techniques. To do this is, in the largest sense, 'church work'.

Women have never been the makers of institutions: they are often accused of not being able to think in terms of rules, pro-cedure, organisation and logical deduction. That is true, and it has been a weakness in women. Organisation has its place in life and so have institutions, but it is a question in the modern world whether these things have not come to occupy too large a place, and even to be a burden to us. When women grow tired of organisations and meetings they go back to their homes and begin again in the way that is a second nature to them, talking in the queue and over the garden fence and bringing in a couple of friends to drink a cup of tea, meeting the children from school and getting to know the teacher and the health visitor and the trades-men. They, in other words, have in their hands most of the slender threads which can re-unite the Church to the local community. Where the woman is at work, there also the Church can be at work through her. Many young Christian women have their husbands' full support: the modern Christian home is a shared responsibility, and the husband rejoices to see his wife using her gifts outside the home and thereby enriching her own contribution to the life of the family.

'The questions you have asked are certainly very interesting,' writes a woman from Berlin in answer to the World Council's questionnaire, 'but please do not be angry if I say that the most important question has not been asked at all. The life of the Church is no longer carried on chiefly through its organisations, but in the houses and families, the factories and offices where Christians meet with others. So the first question should be, What does the Church mean in the lives of women? What chance does the Church give to women to be its representatives at home and in their work?' Women are beginning to answer these questions by experiment in living encounter between the Gospel and their families, friends and work.

INDEX